RAISING
EMOTIONALLY
INTELLIGENT
TEENAGERS

RAISING EMOTIONALLY INTELLIGENT TEENAGERS

■ ■ ■

Parenting with Love, Laughter, and Limits

MAURICE J. ELIAS, PH.D.

STEVEN E. TOBIAS, PSY.D.

BRIAN S. FRIEDLANDER, PH.D.

WITH A FOREWORD BY GOTHAM CHOPRA

Harmony Books • New York

To the memory of Michael Simon Steinberg and in honor of the many other quiet teenage heroes who through their caring, kindness, responsibility, dedication, and humor have exemplified the ideals of the emotionally intelligent adolescent and, by being so, have given so much to their family, friends, and communities.

Published by Harmony Books, New York, New York.
Member of the Crown Publishing Group.

Random House, Inc. New York, Toronto, London, Sydney, Auckland
www.randomhouse.com

HARMONY BOOKS is a registered trademark and the Harmony Books colophon is a trademark of Random House, Inc.

Printed in the United States of America
Design by Debbie Glasserman
Library of Congress Cataloging-in-Publication Data

Elias, Maurice J.
Raising emotionally intelligent teenagers : parenting with love, laughter, and limits /
by Maurice J. Elias, Steven E. Tobias, Brian S. Friedlander.—1st ed.
1. Parent and teenager—United Sates.   2. Teenagers—United States—Psychology.
3. Teenagers—United States—Family relationships.   4. Adolescent psychology—
United States.   I. Tobias, Steven E.   II. Friedlander, Brian S.   III. Title.
HQ799.15.E44   2000
649'.125—dc21   00-029560

ISBN 0-609-60298-5

10 9 8 7 6 5 4 3 2

Contents

PART 3: USING YOUR TOOLS: SOME EXAMPLES FOR THE REAL WORLD 135

Acknowledgments

The authors would like to thank a wonderfully talented literary team that has supported our work: Shaye Areheart, Peter Guzzardi, Vivian Fong, Dina Siciliano, and Wendy Schuman at Crown Publishers/Random House, their many colleagues, and Denise Marcil, our superb literary agent.

MAURICE J. ELIAS

As the years go on, my feeling of debt to family, friends, colleagues, students, coworkers, and other collaborators only grows. My wife, Ellen, and daughters, Sara Elizabeth and Samara Alexandra, are sources of inspiration and grounding. They challenge me and support me, and never let me become complacent. My parents, Agnes and Sol, continue to amaze me and serve as a fountain of stories. I am deeply grateful to my colleagues in the Collaborative to Advance Social and Emotional Learning (www.CASEL.org), the HOPE Foundation (www.communitiesofhope.org), the Center for Social and Emotional Education (www.tc.columbia.edu/academic/psel), the Institute for Emotionally Intelligent Learning in Illinois (DrLaugh01@aol.com), the Social Problem Solving Program of the University of Medicine and Dentistry of New Jersey (www.umdnj.edu/spsweb), 6Seconds on the West Coast (www.6Seconds.org), the Society for Community Research and Action (www.apa.org/divisions/div27), my wonderful colleagues in Israel and their inspiring Binat Halev—"Wisdom of the Heart"—program, the veteran implementers in the Highland Park (N.J.) public schools and at the Children's Institute in Verona, N.J., the "Talking with TJ" Team based in Plainfield, N.J.—the list can go on and on. I apologize for not mentioning everyone, but that would be a book in itself. (You see, Tom, I would include you if you ever got a computer!)

I would like to make one personal acknowledgment, and that is to Dr. Bernard Novick, of blessed memory. Bernie passed away in June 1999. He dedicated his life to youth, to upholding decency and the best of Jewish values and human values, and to helping schools and other organizations function in a humane way that would also allow them to reach their goals. Bernie was fond of saying, "A system is perfectly designed to produce the results that it produces." He also was a champion of truth telling, of the importance of not putting our personal pride or bias ahead of what was needed to do good things for kids. One unfulfilled dream of his was to see Emotional Intelligence find its way into the curriculum and instruction of the Rabbi Pesach Raymon Yeshiva. Under the guidance of Rabbi Gross and the school's Binat Halev Committee, and with the help of Bernie's extraordinary wife and partner, Phyllis, his dream is being realized; many of the ideas in this book are part of that work. I can't begin to quantify how much I have learned from Bernie over the years. I can only thank him and try to carry on some of what he has inspired.

STEVEN E. TOBIAS

My family has certainly been crucial in the development of this book and my other endeavors. My wife, Carol, has been patient and understanding and has, by her sacrifices and support, enabled me to help others. She is also my sounding board and editor. My children, Gillian and Meg, show me through their love what parenting is all about, and their behavior has taught me more about parenting than any professional source possibly could. My colleagues at the Center for Child and Family Development provide me with professional stimulation and friendship. I also want to thank staff members of the Banyan School, Far Hills Country Day

School, Gerrard Berman Day School, and Westmont Montessori for allowing me to learn from them and to be of some assistance in return.

BRIAN S. FRIEDLANDER

When working on a project such as this, it is invigorating to know that there are so many people on your team rooting for you and for its success. As always, I would like to thank my wife, Helene, who has always nurtured my interests and has allowed me the latitude to work on these projects and others, all the while knowing what a sacrifice it is to the family. Your love, commitment, and faith are special gifts which continue to inspire me. I would also like to acknowledge my daughter, Chelsea, who is a source of inspiration even while she good-naturedly allows me to sharpen my parenting skills. I would like to thank my father, Robert, for his continued interest and excitement in my book projects and his marketing skills, and also Rose, who shares in his enthusiasm. To my in-laws, Ruth and Hyman, it is wonderful knowing that you are always there for us. I am deeply thankful for your continued support. To my brother Devin and sister-in-law Sara and their children, Allison, Carly, Melissa, and Mallory, it is wonderful knowing that your love and support are always there. To my sister Susan and brother-in-law David and their children, Jason, Lindsey, and Amanda, thanks for all your support, encouragement, and love. To my brother-in-law Victor and sister-in-law Kathie, thanks for your guidance, love, and for being there for me.

I would also like to thank the Chester Township Public Schools (Chester, N.J.), and Dr. Pamela Fiander, Superintendent of Schools, for their continued support of my professional endeavors. Lastly, I would like to thank my supervisor, Nancy Novack, Director of Special Services, for encouraging me to pursue my interests and for providing a supportive working environment.

Foreword

The Coolest Connection

I have to admit that when I started to write this foreword, I struggled mightily. What could I—a nonparent—say about parenting? I couldn't pretend to be an expert on something for which I had no expertise. I knew instinctively and from the experiences of my own parents that there is perhaps no job quite as difficult as raising a child. And raising a teen presents the most intense challenge of all.

When I wrote my first book, *Child of the Dawn,* a novel about a young teenage orphan boy searching for his place in life, a lot of interviewers would ask me if the book was based on my own upbringing. Though my parents might blanche at the notion of their own son suggesting in any way that he was ever an orphan, my answer was this: almost all teens, in fact, all people, endure times of feeling abandoned and/or lost in a world that can suddenly seem strange and unfamiliar.

I think, inside of us, we all harbor some orphan-like insecurities, some sense that we must find our place in this world on our own. And for teens, this impulse toward alienation and abandonment often comes on quickly and without warning.

And though I lack the experience of having raised a teenager, I think I've witnessed some pretty good parenting from "the other side." Ideally, good parenting begin with preparing a teen for the multitude of choices that suddenly begin to present themselves. But the very best parenting is required when things have already gone haywire. From a kid's perspective, that's because the teenage years are full of firsts—the first exposure to drugs and alcohol, the first relationships, and the first "adult" responsibilities. I know as well as anyone that it's cool to feel in control, but eventually teenagers are going to screw up. They're going to break the rules—it's just the way they're wired.

But, on a path full of potential hazards, where the inevitability of screwing up is certain, the real question is What are teens searching for? In an attempt to answer that question, I'll share a story:

Recently, I attended a youth rally for the Pope in St. Louis. About 20,000 teenagers were in attendance, rocking and rolling for hours to a number of bands before the Pope even arrived. I was covering the event for the news organization for which I work, so my crew and I were trying to figure out our "angle" by walking around the stadium and observing the goings on. The first thing that struck me as strange were the throngs of teenagers jamming and dancing while waiting to hear the "Holy Father."

I started to ask random kids if they were Catholic. Soon, as a TV camera tends to do, we had drawn a big group of assorted teenagers. It turned out that about 70 percent of them were indeed Catholics, but the others had either come with Catholic friends or just "to hang out." When I asked the Catholics if they considered themselves very religious, if they followed all the "rules" for being Catholic, they immediately knew what I was talking about. "Not really, man," one of the older guys answered with a sly smile. "Rules are for the hardcore followers. And a lot of us just aren't that way."

"But it's not just about the rules," a girl next to him added. I asked the crowd of kids why they were there if they weren't hardcore believers.

A teenager pushed himself forward through the group. "'Cuz it's cool, man. Because he's the Pope—he's our Holy Father; it's just cool to feel connected."

Connected, that's what teenagers want to be. We live in a world where kids are forced to grow up faster than ever before. Teenagers are exposed to all sorts of things from a stupefying number of sources, and it's pretty easy to get lost in it all. And when the seas get really rough, when tempests roll through in the form of toxic temptations and real adult responsibilities, it's critical to have anchors to hang onto. The best anchor is a parent who's willing simply to be there—a parent who is willing to be present in an *emotionally intelligent* way.

In the following pages, you will be exposed to some extraordinary techniques that will help you and your teenager create the most precious part of your relationship thus far. My favorites—accrued via direct experience—are learning to laugh with your parents, learning to communicate through simple rituals like reading a chapter together *from this book,* and last, but definitely not least, understanding how to make *spirituality* an elemental part of a teen's identity development.

But these rituals and disciplines should come with a warning attached. Rules, rituals, and disciplines are worth nothing unless the intention behind them comes from a strong-willed, loving, and flexible place.

It's become too cliché to say that a parent needs to be a best friend. And it's not always true; parents have to play a number of roles in order to raise a teen successfully, including being the disciplinarian and/or the villain at times. But they must also frequently be partners who are willing to play the roles of confidante, listener, conspirator, and playmate.

From early in my childhood, my parents told me that even though I had been born into their family—sharing distinctive biological traits with them—I was not theirs. I was a gift from the universe. They would take care of me until I was ready and able to give a gift back to the universe. They also let me know that while they were the caretakers this time, someday—if not in this lifetime, perhaps in the next—our roles might switch. Spiritually we are all just transients passing through. Today I'm the son, tomorrow I'll be the father. In the course of our lives, we all play different roles. We are all indeed ancient souls, here for some precious little time to share some stories, secrets, and adventures together.

Raising Emotionally Intelligent Teenagers pays homage to this idea by asking parents to not let their adolescent's intellect be the focus of their parenting or their relationship with their child. A teenager's emotional and spiritual well-being is at the core of his or her identity. When a teen is growing up in a healthy and stable environment, it is this emotionally and spiritually nourished part of them that fuels their ability to give back to the universe—with the result that all of us benefit.

So, if you can recognize, above all else, that the labels "parent" and "child" are simply temporary assignments in the most precious of partnerships, then reading and integrating the messages in *Raising Emotionally Intelligent Teenagers* will put you on the path to making a parent-teen connection that is "cool" beyond compare.

—*Gotham Chopra*

Part 1

■   ■   ■

PREPARE YOURSELF
TO RAISE
AN EMOTIONALLY
INTELLIGENT
TEENAGER

Chapter 1

Parenting by Choice and Not by Chance
Applying Emotionally Intelligent Parenting
in Hectic Times

Parenthood is an endless series of small events, periodic conflicts, and sudden crises which call for a response. The response is not without consequence: it affects personality for better or worse. Our teenager's character is shaped by experience with people and situations. Character education requires presence that demonstrates and contact that communicates.

We want our teenager to be a "mensch," a human being with compassion, commitment, and courage, a person whose life is guided by a core of strength and a code of fairness. To achieve these humane goals, we need humane methods. Love is not enough. Insight is insufficient. Good parents need skill.

—Dr. Haim Ginott, *Between Parent and Teenager*

Is your life hectic? Did you plan for it to be this way? Did you sit down two years ago and say, Wow, my life is so relaxed, I have so much time that over the next two years, I want to greatly increase how many things my kids—and we—are doing?

The hectic lives that most of us lead are not the result of careful planning. It just happened. With all this activity comes more and more stress, and less time with our kids. Think about it. Often, even when you are with your kids, there is a part of you that is still thinking about where you just left, and another part of you that is thinking about what you will be doing next. It's hard to be fully present for them. We have a lot on our minds, including planning how to get our kids to where they have to be next and how to get ourselves to where we have to be, and we rush around and worry about whether our arrangements will work out. Like it or not, our kids pick up on this. And often their reaction is to believe that they are not very high on their parents' list of priorities.

This is a very demanding time during which to be a parent of a teenager. Maybe the only thing more difficult is to be a teenager! There are more influences than ever on them, and more sources of distraction. James Comer, M.D., a renowned educator and the author of *Waiting for a Miracle: Schools Can't Solve Our Problems, but We Can*, observes that never before in human history has there been so much information going directly to children unfiltered by adult caregivers. This is more important than it might seem at first—so read it again! It means that parents are now in serious competition for the attention of their children, and our attempts to influence them are constantly being diluted by numerous messages encouraging them to act and think differently from ways we would like them to.

A parent's time is extremely precious and pressured. Our hectic lives create barriers to entering our teens'"other world"—even if they would let us in. As James Comer has alerted us, they are under the influence of their peers, the media, the Internet, and who knows what else. Though we don't have unlimited energy for parenting, it's something we have to deal with in an emotionally intelligent manner...and we can!

ON THE ROAD TO ADULTHOOD

To do so requires that we look carefully at the teenage years, especially at how they are today and how they will be in the foreseeable future. On the journey from childhood to adulthood, adolescence represents the bridge. How are our teenagers going to travel over that bridge? What roads will they take? Given all the demands on our time, what are the best ways to guide our teens in a positive direction?

Adolescence is a process, not an end product or even a stop

along the highway of life. Kids pass through it at high speed. Our job as parents is to make sure they get to the real goal of being an emotionally intelligent adult with as few accidents along the way as possible and to help them when they hit a pothole or two and have a problem. You are not trying to raise a Superteen, because a Superteen will not necessarily end up as an emotionally well-adjusted and successful adult. Adolescence is for learning how to become an adult, not for learning how to become a successful adolescent.

Now, let's also be realistic. It is not easy to have an impact on your adolescents, especially if you don't already have a great relationship with them. We are strong believers in realistic simplification. What are the most important things that parents can do, consistently, that can make a very big difference in preparing adolescents for competence in adulthood? Many books give page after page of advice, on many different topics. These often sound terrific, especially to those who have the leisure time to read and think about them—such as people without kids in their homes! But in our professional experience, there is only so much that parents can do, are willing to do, and can keep track of. We want to make that minimum as strong and as impactful as possible.

WHAT DO WE WANT FOR OUR TEENAGERS?

There are certain directions toward which parents want teens to head. We want them to be knowledgeable, responsible, nonviolent, and caring... is there a parent who does not want this for his or her children? Not that we have met, but, after all, it takes just this combination of qualities for our children to be able to support us in our retirement years, of course! More important, it takes these same skills for our kids to grow up to be successful, productive citizens of their schools, families, workplaces, and communities.

How do we help our teenagers reach these goals? It's a journey that parents and teens have been taking for years but now must take in a way that reflects our changing times. It's not another "new millennium" thing, but it is the result of forces that got rolling in the 1990s and are not about to stop.

LOVE, LAUGHTER, AND LIMITS

It requires, on our part, a balance of Love, Laughter, and Limits... and another L, which we will mention in a moment. Love, Laughter, and Limits provide a map for parenting our teenagers on a road that has many curves, lots of bumps, but also many miles of beautiful scenery.

Love, Laughter, and Limits. Can parenting of teenagers be that simple? Well, our answer is both no and yes. We say no because we know how much is involved with parenting. We are parents, with children ranging in age from eight to twenty. We work with hundreds of families and dozens and dozens of schools. We see the difficulties and the frustrations, but we also see the joys and successes. Nothing about parenting is simple. But we also say yes because we know that parents today need to have a focus for how they raise their teenagers, and they need to do so with "emotional intelligence." Focus is necessary because most of us lead lives that are packed with activity.

And this leads to our fourth L: Linkages. Teenagers need to grow up at least as ready for interdependence as for independence. They are going to find themselves working in teams and in groups. They are going to find that the consumer pressures in their lives will leave an emotional and perhaps a spiritual void. We, as parents, may find that we are not able to do as much for our teens as we might like, or they might need. Here is our quick summary of these four L's:

LOVE

Caring relationships form the foundation of family life and cooperation. Without this, parents often have only economic and punitive leverage to use with their teens. And these are not ideal strategies.

LAUGHTER

Emotions affect how and what we do and are willing to do. Positive emotions are essential for healthy adolescent growth. Humor is not frivolous; it's the ultimate psychic vitamin.

LIMITS

Limits are not about restriction as much as they are about focus and direction and setting boundaries. The skills parents and children possess in goal setting and problem solving help keep teens on course and turn good ideas into constructive actions.

LINKAGES

Teenagers need to be contributors more than consumers, and to belong more than to buy. In a world of increasing complexity and sophistication, parents cannot expect to "do all" and "be all" for their teens. Our ability to help them make healthy connections will be at least as important as things we do for and with them directly.

There is a lot more to this that we will go over. For now, we want to give you an overview of some of the main things we need to do with our teens, and why. Then we will spend the bulk of this book with practical, parent-tested, emotionally intelligent ways "how." We don't want to give you more than you can use, but we want to give you enough so that you have choices and can find approaches that fit your circumstances, children, and style. Above all, we want to help you engage in parenting by choice, not by chance.

PARENTING BY CHOICE, NOT BY CHANCE

We view Love, Laughter, Limits, and Linkages as the core, the center of parenting. Many things in our busy lives, including multiple inputs about parenting, obscure that core. For us to keep within the guardrails and work effectively with our teenagers, we need to act with emotional intelligence. We must balance the impulses of our emotions and the logic of the situations in front of us. We must learn to read our own feelings and the unfolding circumstances and relationships around us accurately and inform our actions with these perspectives. In a few moments, we will provide a "refresher" on emotional intelligence, based on the work begun by Daniel Goleman in his book of that name and continued by us in *Emotionally Intelligent Parenting*. Both Dan Goleman's book and ours have found their way into numerous international editions, speaking to what seems to be a universal recognition that human behavior and relationships must be informed by both the head and the heart.

The particular areas that define Emotionally Intelligent Parenting are these:

1. Show awareness of your own feelings and those of others.
2. Show empathy and try to understand others' points of view.
3. Keep your cool and follow the 24-Karat Golden Rule.
4. Be positive and be goal and plan oriented.
5. Use your BEST social skills in handling relationships.

We discuss these areas later as providing parents with the tools for **ESP: Evaluating** and sizing up situations, feelings, and perspectives of those involved and inhibiting our own tendencies to act too quickly, extremely, or unkindly; **Selecting** goals and planning a positive and constructive course of action; and **Proceeding** with sound social skills—we will explain what we mean by BEST—in the context of building and maintaining positive relationships. Emotionally Intelligent Parenting is a tool for helping bring Love, Laughter, Limits, and Linkages into everyday family life, and a way of interacting with our teenagers in numerous situations so that their own skills in the area of emotional intelligence are enhanced.

PREPARING TEENAGERS FOR THE FUTURE

We have talked about the parents, but we also need to keep focused on our teenagers. Magazines print regular surveys of teens, all about what's wrong with them, what we need to do for them, and how they are growing up too fast, too violent, too selfish, too whatever. While the situations in which we are raising teenagers truly are different now because of the growing number of influences on their development and the hecticness of everyday life, teenagers are still kids making a transition to adulthood. We run a risk when we start to believe all the hype we are reading. Our view is this: Situations are changing but kids are kids, and teens are teens. How do we keep focused on what they need and make sure that the tail of pop culture does not wag the dog of parenting? If we are to parent by choice and not by chance, we have to take out our road maps of adolescent development and be sure we are focused on the main routes and destinations, rather than the billboards, minor detours, and cosmetic face-lifts along the side of the road.

None of us can predict with great confidence the adult world our teenagers, especially those in their early teens, will enter five or ten years from now. We would have been hard-pressed to imagine the present world of jobs and economies based on our knowledge ten years ago. And there is a sense that things are changing even more rapidly. But kids' development is not subject to such fast changes. Parents of teens need to set their compasses on building their teens' assets in the following areas:

1. *Appreciation*, the feeling of being loved, valued, and cared for and about;

2. *Belonging,* being grounded in meaningful social groups, identifying with important goals and values, and growing through diverse contacts and relationships;

3. *Competencies and Confidence,* which come from having the skills of social and emotional intelligence needed to manage in a social world, to resist harmful impulses, to respond with awareness to social opportunities and pressures, to build and maintain positive relationships in the family, the workplace, and the community, to enact roles essential for citizenship, and to make valued contributions; and

4. *Contributions,* a sense that one matters, that beyond oneself is a larger world of relationships, ideals, and causes to which one is truly connected.

These areas—A, B, and the three C's—can be put in various orders. In fact, they are interconnected. We can think of them as tires on a car—all essential, all needing to be in alignment and with good tread—or we can think of them as parts of one wheel, parts that must be in balance, fully inflated, and not disproportionate in size or shape, which would keep the wheel from rolling smoothly. We will draw on both types of analogies, and you might well think of your own. But be sure your analogy is dynamic and includes the reality that not all things go smoothly and that constant attention and regular adjustment are the norm.

PUTTING IT ALL TOGETHER
TO CREATE AN OASIS AGAINST STRESS:
MORE ENJOYABLE THAN YOU MIGHT THINK

As we have said already and you will see in this book, we feel strongly about the importance of humor. Life is serious, our lives are serious, and the risks to our teenagers are serious, but to approach parenting too seriously is to keep steering straight when the road is curving. We must admit that we cannot predict or control everything. We cannot provide everything. We are less able than ever to protect and shield our children from danger and difficulty. Time with our kids is highly limited and pressured. How we grew up is not necessarily the best guide to how our teens should grow up.

So, let's parent with emotional intelligence. Let's be smart but keep focused on having a positive relationship with our teens. Let's make our home an expanding oasis of peace in a desert of pressure and stress. We all need that oasis. You know this as an adult. If that oasis is not at home, teens will seek it out elsewhere. Our home needs to be that oasis or at least be linked to it. If not, to paraphrase Professor Harold Hill in *The Music Man*, there'll be trouble in River City, trouble with a capital T that rhymes with D, that stands for Disconnection.

Our teens are in the most trouble when they are not connected with parents, family, school, workplace, leisure, or positive peers. The way to prevent disconnection is to build our teens' assets, to invest in their strengths at least as much as, if not more than, we correct their weaknesses. Lots of self-correction takes place when teens feel appreciation, contribution, competence and confidence, and positive belonging.

A REFRESHER ON THE PRINCIPLES OF EMOTIONALLY INTELLIGENT PARENTING

Whether you have read *Emotional Intelligence* or *Emotionally Intelligent Parenting* or simply have communed with these books in the friendly confines of a bookstore without taking them home, we want to review with you via our E.Q. Family Quiz, created in collaboration with Gay Norton Edelman, senior editor for special features at *McCall's* magazine. There are two parts, one for you to do concerning your teenagers (as well as other children) and one for you to do on yourself. For each question, give yourself 3 points if the answer is Definitely True; 2 points for Sometimes/Sort of True; and 1 point for Rarely, If Ever True. Here we go:

Does Your Child:

___   know lots of words to describe her feelings

___   talk easily about emotions

___   have empathy and sympathy for others

___   have an optimistic attitude

___   wait patiently for something he really wants

___   have goals reasonable for her age and some thoughts about how to reach those goals

___   listen attentively

___   know what he needs and how to ask for it

___   know how to solve problems independently

___   handle herself well in a group of kids her own age

As a Parent, Do You:

___   know what you are feeling most of the time

___   regularly share your feelings with others

___   try to understand someone else's point of view, even if in the middle of an argument

___   have an optimistic, hopeful outlook

___   find time to laugh with loved ones

___   control your temper when you are stressed

___   know how to listen carefully and restate what has just been said

___   consider many options when making a decision

___   have goals and plans for achieving them

___   know how to make connections with people to help to fulfill your children's needs

Scoring

Add up the scores for each section separately.

10–15   Your child needs (or you need) E.Q. time every day

16–24   Your child is (or you are) in okay shape. But don't rest on your laurels—more improvements can be made.

25+   Your child is (or you are) an E.Q. star whose emotional savvy lights up their own lives and the life of others

Many aspects of Emotionally Intelligent Parenting relate to you, your teenagers, and your relationships with one another. The quiz is one way of focusing on certain areas that you can see easily apply to everyday life and family interaction. The ten aspects we presented are drawn from the five areas of Emotionally Intelligent Parenting presented in detail by Dan Goleman in *Emotional Intelligence* and by us in *Emotionally Intelligent Parenting*. As you may have noticed earlier, we have reworded them slightly for application to teenagers. Below we present each of the five areas, along with a quick review of the main features:

1. BE AWARE OF ONE'S OWN FEELINGS AND THOSE OF OTHERS

One of the most frequently asked questions is "How are you?" It's how we initiate most telephone conversations and many of our first contacts with others, but it usually is just a greeting. It is, however, one of the most important questions we can be asked. Whether we choose to answer or not, we need to know how we are feeling and how to put words to our feelings in a way that reflects their great variety.

Teenagers who are not able to reflect on and accurately label their feelings find themselves at a distinct social, academic, and vocational disadvantage. Imagine not being able to distinguish being bored from being mad, upset from sad, or glad from proud. We would wind up acting inappropriately in many situations. Since how we believe we feel will influence how we act, teenagers who are sad tend to mope or withdraw. When they are happy, they are likely to spread their cheer. When they are in a boring situation but act angry instead, trouble is likely. And the same is true of their parents, of course!

An obviously related issue is being aware of others' feelings. Interactions with others go better when you are on their emotional wavelength. This requires us to know the signs of feelings in others and how to accurately label them. Knowing when to ask a teacher for an extension or when to ask someone for a date are matters of considerable practical significance to many teens. And teens would like their parents to be as discerning in knowing when to ask them to do chores around the house (never!) as they are in knowing when to ask their employers for a raise.

2. SHOW EMPATHY AND TRY TO UNDERSTAND OTHERS' POINTS OF VIEW

Empathy is the capacity to share in another's feelings. It helps, of course, if one is skilled at being aware of both one's own feelings and those of others. Very much related is being able to know how another person sees something. Indeed, empathy has been referred to as seeing something through another's eyes or, as the sage Hillel said centuries ago, "Do not judge others until you stand in their shoes." That is not easy to do! Yet understanding another's point of view *and* his or her feelings about what is happening is a big part of what defines us as human beings.

Among the skills involved are careful listening and reading the nonverbal body language and tone of voice that often convey more than our words. One way of understanding empathy is as a nonverbal emotional understanding of others. But empathy involves other skills as well. Cognitive ability matters, as does one's range of life experiences. Teenagers who have grown up with television, videos, and movie trailers on their computers tend to draw upon these media as if they were reflective of something other than the life experiences of the creators of those media. Our view is that teens act more mature than they truly are because they are exposed to so many "life experiences" in a shallow and impersonal way, through television and videos.

Young children (and immature adults) tend to view the world in terms of their own wants and needs. As kids get older, around age seven or eight, they become better able to negotiate, compromise, and be tolerant. Whether these abilities become refined and part of your teenager's personality depends on their experiences taking and dealing with others' perspectives. As we will mention later, service opportunities are among the most valuable and potent ways to build empathy and experience a wide range of perspectives, and there are things parents can do to encourage such occurrences.

3. KEEP YOUR COOL AND FOLLOW THE 24-KARAT GOLDEN RULE

How impulsive is your teen? How good at waiting are you? These areas were part of our quiz; they reflect important research findings that healthier and more successful children are those who are able to control their impulses to have or do what is right there in front of them, for greater reward later. We know this in part from the Marshmallow Test. As recounted most visibly by Dan Goleman in *Emotional Intelligence*, researcher Walter Mischel conducted an experiment in which young children were told that they would be left alone and if they wanted to, they could have the marshmallow that was on the table. *But* if they waited until a researcher came back into the room, they could have two marshmallows. Being able to wait turns out to be associated with better results on a variety of psychological and behavioral indicators. Most remarkable is that, years later, kids who waited tended to score 200 points better on their SATs, the academic-skills test so important for college entry.

What does this mean? It means it's often helpful to keep your cool and not act on every impulse. We hear some of you already: What about spontaneity? Are we trying to make everyone into robots? This sounds like Vulcan intelligence, not emotional intelligence. Okay, okay—go have a milk shake and leave us alone!

Seriously, we are trying our best to ground this book in realism. The issue is one of balance. We are human, and we are going to act on impulses, hunches, and whims. We can't imagine how to stop this, nor would we want to. But many educators and parents are seeing a generation of teenagers who want to do it all and do it now. Many seem to have too little patience with what it takes to delve into a project to a serious, in-depth degree, especially when it's outside their own areas of special interest.

We are seeing the effects of a surfing culture—not California, catch-a-wave stuff, but couch potato, TV remote-control, and Internet surfing stuff. Teenagers, and in some cases their parents, are too often in a "scanning" mode. Without even realizing it, we are developing habits of moving quickly, looking less carefully, waiting for shorter periods, and being less patient. Hence, we want to make sure that this imbalance does not keep shifting, and thus we urge parents to try to "keep your cool."

The second part of this area refers to the 24-Karat Golden Rule:

> **Do unto your children as you would have
> other people do unto your children.**

The common Golden Rule, "Do unto others as you would have others do unto you," we must admit, has been around for a while and seems to have served the world pretty well. But we feel something more powerful is needed by parents of teenagers as we embark on the twenty-first century. With our lives being so hectic and stressed, a moment of honest reflection might reveal times when we have said and done things to our own children for which, if an outsider tried them, we would want them arrested and imprisoned.

"But it's not a problem," you're saying. "Our kids know we don't mean it. And they also know we do it out of love." Yeah, and it was just a slight addition and rounding error that we made on our tax returns. If we don't mean it, why say it? And if we wanted to show our teenagers love and we gave them a choice between hearing us say something unkind to them out of our own stress and anger or getting a twenty-dollar bill, what do you think they'd choose? "I really want to hear that put-down, but I am going to take the money, out of love."

The 24-Karat Golden Rule asks that we take our teens' perspectives with empathy, control our own impulses, and know when we are overwhelmed and not take this out on our kids. It's easy to say but very hard to do. One way to be more successful is to "look at your teenager through rose-colored glasses." Keep their strengths in mind. When you look at them, look at them with Love and Laughter, not Limits. See their best possibilities and speak to them as if those possibilities are fragile and might not come to pass if your teens' confidence in themselves and in you is eroded. It helps, of course, that what we are saying happens to be true. Positives from parents propel teens forward.

How Can This Really Help My Teenager? Keeping your cool and following the 24-Karat Golden Rule is more important for teenagers than you might at first think. Strong anger, frustration, anxiety, sadness, and similar emotions interfere with teens' learning. (Actually, they interfere with anyone's learning.) When kids hear hurtful things from their caregivers, they are less able to focus on their responsibilities, whether at school, at home, or on the job. However, we can offset these hurts by helping our children experience strong positive feelings, often by encouraging them to use, and be recognized for, valued strengths. Then we will find that our teenagers are more able to manage impulsive behavior, relate positively to others individually and in groups, and develop empathy and the ability to take others' perspectives. These are skills essential to academic, career, and life advancement.

What Can We Do to Bring the 24-Karat Golden Rule into Our Family? Don't wait another minute. Put a chart on your refrigerator or take a notebook and mark down, each day, any time that parents or other adult caregivers in your household violate the 24-Karat Golden Rule and say something in the heat of strong emotions that was not what was really meant. Also keep track of any time the adults restrained themselves from saying something that they might otherwise have said. Count it even if you started to say something and quickly stopped yourself, and count it double if you find yourself enhancing a strength that your teen has. See if you can improve yourself by the end of the week.

Coping with behavioral impulses is also important for obvious reasons. Instinctive behavioral responses to a conflict situation are often ineffective in coping with that problem. As human beings, we are wired to react with a fight-or-flight response to problem situations. In prehistoric times, this was helpful to our survival. However, neither fighting nor running away usually serves us well in modern society. We have to use the information we have about our own and others' feelings and perspectives to help us better control our impulses. And then we have to start thinking further ahead.

4. BE POSITIVE AND BE GOAL AND PLAN ORIENTED

We have come to believe in the tremendous power of optimism, hope, and humor. That's why we put Love, Laughter, and Limits in this book's subtitle. There is a distinct biochemistry to hopefulness and positive spirits, including improved blood flow, cardiovascular and aerobic efficiency, immune system activity, and stress-level reduction. Laughter, to us, is more than chuckles and guffaws, as we will discuss later. Laughter is linked to our creativity and inventiveness, and these, of course, are linked to our ability to be clear about our goals and to solve problems in new ways and make plans to see our ideas come to fruition; in so doing, we change the world.

Maybe this seems overly dramatic to you. But the families with which we have worked have indeed had their relationships with their teens and, for all practical purposes, their whole worlds change because they learned about Love, Laughter, and Limits, as well as Linkages. Part of what makes us distinctly human is our capacity to set goals and make plans to reach those goals. But we must do so in an emotionally intelligent way, keeping in mind the feelings and perspectives of others involved and sometimes, as parents, keeping our views to ourselves a little longer so we can listen more carefully and deeply to our teenagers and make our decisions and plans with greater insight.

Part of being positive is to recognize that all members of our family, including ourselves and our teens, are always learning. To learn effectively in our current, hectic society, we need to get feedback, from time to time, about how our efforts are doing. Are we setting goals wisely, and do our plans reach them? This book includes tools to keep track of ways we try to solve problems, ways to judge how well they work, and things we can do to improve across a variety of situations. "Where will I find the time to do any tracking?" we are often asked. Indeed, parents (and teens) are so busy so much of the time that self-reflection seems like it is not "productive enough" to be worth our time. There is a familiar auto parts commercial that sums up our response: Parents can pay now or pay later. Based on what we know about Emotionally Intelligent Parenting, there is no "easy" way, and so we will present you with various approaches to improve parenting through feedback.

5. USE YOUR BEST SOCIAL SKILLS IN HANDLING RELATIONSHIPS

Do you always act your BEST in situations with you teenagers? BEST stands for:

Body posture
Eye contact
Saying the right words (and skipping the wrong words)
Tone of voice

We speak volumes to our teenagers in the way we approach them and the care we use when talking to them. Of course, there are cultural factors that define, more or less, appropriate ways to do things. And our teens also let us know which of our little habits drive them up the wall. Do you do any of these?

Body: challenging, disinterested, not facing teen when speaking
Eyes: rolling your eyes in disbelief

Saying: calling them by a name they don't like, talking about
  them in the third person even when they are present for the
  conversation ("Maybe Steven wants some broccoli." "I am sitting right here, Mom, and I hate broccoli. I'm a Republican.")
Tone: sarcastic, bossy, demanding, condescending

If you do any or all of these, then you need some improvement
in being your BEST. When we are at our BEST, we are like a car
with new radial tires. We are right on top of our conversations
and interactions, gripping every curve and responding smoothly
to every bump. We convey to the people we are with that we
respect them and want to be there with them, communicating
meaningfully.

Another way we put our BEST skills to work is when we are
part of groups. As parents want their family to function well as a
group, they also should want their teenagers to grow up with
skills for contributing to groups at school, on the job, and in community life. Learning to listen to others carefully and accurately,
to take turns, to harmonize different feelings, to compromise, to
create consensus, and to state one's ideas clearly are among many
social skills that help us work better in groups. And, of course,
when members use these skills, groups—including families—
work better. Modeling matters a great deal. A related and important social skill is the ability to "bounce back" constructively
when we hit inevitable roadblocks and obstacles in our dealings
with others. You will read more about BEST in Part 2.

HOW IMPORTANT IS THIS REALLY?

Parents who are engaged in Emotionally Intelligent Parenting
focus on the above principles in their own parenting and encourage the development of these principles in their children, both at
home and in school. They are concerned about giving children
the skills needed for success in life, not just in academics. Emo-

tionally Intelligent Parenting draws its power from the way in which it becomes part of your everyday household and parenting routine. It leads to small, positive changes in our relationships with our children that are repeated day after day. Further, the approach is grounded in research and advances in understanding how the human brain works and the role of emotion in learning and memory.

WILL IT HELP THEM LEARN BETTER?

Our emotions strongly affect how and what we learn. When teenagers, whose emotions can be quite powerful, experience anger, frustration, anxiety, sadness, or similar emotions, their learning is not as efficient or effective. Children who hurt are less able to learn than those who do not. What we have also discovered, however, is the power of positive feelings and of teenagers' using and being appreciated for valued strengths. Emotionally Intelligent Parenting asks parents to focus on children's strengths while also giving children the skills they'll need to manage impulsive behavior, relate positively to others individually and in groups, and develop empathy and the ability to take others' perspectives. These competencies underlie success in all human endeavors and most certainly are vital to academic, career, civic, and life advancement.

WHAT'S NEXT AFTER REFRESHMENT?

You have taken the quiz and you have had some refreshment. You probably already have some ideas about how to bring a little more emotional intelligence into your parenting. And all for less than the price of two theater tickets, even at a big discount! But we have lots more for you. Next, we are going to move on to something old and new: Love, Laughter, Limits, and Linkages.

Why are these so critical for our teenagers? How does it help them meet their essential developmental needs? To answer those questions we will revisit A, B, and the three C's: Appreciation, Belonging, Competencies and Confidence, and Contributions. We will show you how these are the wheels that will keep your teenagers' search for identity on a sound road.

In Chapter 4, we will take a look at how to make your house an oasis against stress and a place where laughter can be heard, or at least smiles seen. Chapter 5 is a transitional chapter. You will have read the basic principles, and Part 2 presents the tools for putting all of our ideas into action. But the most important tool is you. Are you ready? Have you looked into your past and into your present situation to make sure you are ready for providing Love, Laughter, Limits, and Linkages in an emotionally intelligent manner? Have you gotten sufficiently past issues of your own upbringing and adolescence? We will help you take a painless, lighthearted, and useful look.

Part 2 lays out the tool kit needed to tune our parenting engines, and Part 3 is filled with examples of how parents have used the tools to go down the parenting road with their teenagers. It's a little like the Chicken Soup approach, but with Emotionally Intelligent Parenting ingredients. We provide stories and vignettes with parent-child dialogues to help you see how the tools are used in real-world, complicated situations. We also include a chapter we call "The Clinical Corner," to help you understand the fuzzy boundaries between teenage behavior that is unusual and that which is worrisome, and between behavior that is eccentric and that which is scary. There certainly are times when getting a professional opinion on what is happening is quite useful.

Our final chapter is for parents and teens to read together. Yes, parents, get your teens and learn about one another, as we reveal in writing here, for the first time, secrets about teens and parents that heretofore were only part of the oral tradition, if that. Warning: If you wind up taking this unserious chapter too seriously, we are going to recommend you for a Dr. Dunkelblau Down-Up

Over-and-Under Loop-de-Loop Out-Your-Ear Through-the-Eyeball Spot-Laser Supercalifragilistic Humor Implant...a bloodless but money-siphoning experience covered by every medical plan on Jupiter, but none here on Earth. Okay, you are now ready to proceed!

Chapter 2

Love, Laughter, Limits, and Linkages
How to Build a Respectful Relationship with Your Teenager

Remember when your teenager was a baby? You would embrace that baby and gaze into his or her eyes and say, "I can't wait until you get older so I can forbid your use of the car, nag you about your room, make you get off the phone, restrict you for forgetting to do your homework, and ground you for going to a party where there was liquor."

That's not what you said to your infant? Guess what—some of our teenagers think this is exactly what it was like!

What happened to your dreams of parenting? What were you hoping your relationship with your teenager would be like? Is being a parent what you thought it would be?

We all need to reconnect with our parenting dreams. Here are some more questions to help you with your reflections:

What would go into the highlight reel of your parenting experiences thus far? What was your favorite thing about parenting your child or children at the age of:

infancy?
preschool?
elementary school?
middle school?
high school?

Are these the story of your parenting? Or are these sidebars to another story? What is the story of your parenting? What do you want your story to be?

Is being a parent of a teenager what you thought it would be? Is the mix of children you have what you thought it would be like?

There is no script for your parenting story. You author your story most through your deeds, but you also create it through your dreams. Too often, our dreams get lost in the crush of reality, the speed of our lives, the happenstance of situations we did not want or ask for but had to face and have not really bounced back from.

Reflections like these are very important. We would like you to do more than just reflect, though. Please take a moment to write down your responses and reactions—on a piece of paper, in a notebook, in your Palm Pilot, on your computer—or to speak them into a tape recorder or computer. It's worth your time because of the way in which our hectic lives have often diluted our early hopes and wishes. And we would like you to share these reflections with others who are deeply involved in raising your teenager, who care the way you do about how this precious child grows up and makes his or her mark on the world.

When you reconnect with your dreams for your child, and for what you hoped parenting would be, you will find yourself ready to learn about Love, Laughter, Limits, and Linkages. In fact, we suspect that the correct word is not *learn*. We think it will be *rediscover*, because if you have reflected, then you probably have arrived at these as the essentials for parenting teens in these turbulent times.

LOVE

Parents need to convey their love and caring in ways that are clear to their teenager. Parenting that occurs outside of the context of a caring relationship will be a source of stress and frustration. We put love first because without it, the rest has a different meaning. Many people care about teenagers. Teachers do, coaches do, employers do, and certainly retailers and advertisers do. But the caring of parents, and, hopefully, grandparents, is special when it is accompanied by love. Uri Bronfenbrenner, well-known developmental psychologist at Cornell University, refers to an "irrational" feeling of support, despite whatever specifics a child does, as essential for positive growth.

It almost feels odd to have to "make a case" for the importance of love, but actually, what is necessary in parenting now is for parents to reflect very carefully on how they show their love and how they can be sure that their message is getting through.

SHOWING AFFECTION

In what ways do you show affection to your teen? Do you write loving (as contrasted with businesslike) notes? Do you put your arm around your teenager? How often do you say "I love you"? Do you give hugs? How about trying a cyberhug, an electronic hug of different types, modeled after our Box of Hugs in *Emotionally Intelligent Parenting*? This is something that you send via E-mail. Some electronic-card companies now have specific hug cards you can send, especially since the invention of National Hug Day (it occurs in January). But you can send your own. Be creative! Here is a basic cyberhug: ♥you♥.

Here are some others you can try:

CYBERHUG AND A COOKIE: ♥you♥ + 🍪
CYBERHUG AND A HUM: ♥you♥ + ♫
CYBERHUG AND A PRAYER: ♥you♥ + 🛐
CYBERHUG AND A REAL HUG OF YOUR CHOICE WHEN WE SEE EACH
    OTHER: ♥you♥ + 🔲you
CYBERHUG AND A HOP: ♥you♥ + 💃
DOUBLE CYBERHUG: ♥you♥♥you♥
CYBERHUG AND A MUG: ♥you♥+ ☕ (Treat yourself)

Following are some other ways you can show a little more affection to your teenager.

CELEBRATING ACCOMPLISHMENTS

What happens when your teenager does something special? Some examples are: performing in a school play or concert, an after-school performance, involvement in a sporting event, participating in a club or youth group, volunteer activity, or writing something for a newspaper, magazine, or contest. What about a special accomplishment, such as winning a competition of some kind, or participating in one and doing well though not winning? What about smaller acts of kindness within the family? How about milestone events, special birthdays, holiday gatherings, and participation? There are occasions when some parents show special acknowledgment, gather other family members and other families together, and show their pride in their teenager—not necessarily contingent on "winning" as much as participating.

SHARING SPECIAL MOMENTS

What would you say are special moments that you share with your teenager? There are times when, even without words, it is clear that tremendous warmth and love are flowing between you and your teenager. What are these times for you? In some families, they occur during outdoor events, such as hikes, bike rides, or runs. For others, they happen while watching a favorite television program, movie, or sporting event. Still other families find this closeness in shared physical activity, such as painting, building something, even running certain errands. And sometimes these moments are the quiet ones, while parents and teens are walking in a park, attending a religious service, watching a sunrise, a sunset, a thunderstorm, the waves crashing on the shore, or birds in flight. Parents recognize that it is often "easier" to have special moments with younger children, such as while reading to them or holding them in some way. It is no less important for parents and teens, but it certainly is a bit more challenging.

As you consider these possibilities and how they fit with your family situation, we believe it is essential that you give yourself permission to show love to your teenager. And we give you two warnings:

1. Don't show love with the expectation of reciprocation.
2. Don't wait to show love until your teenager "deserves" it— gets good grades, finally cleans their room, talks nicely to you, and so on.

Show love because you want to show love and because you know it is the right thing to do, *not* because you want love in return or as a "reward" for doing what you want. It's always easier to keep giving when one is receiving in return and to give when everything is really rosy. But part of the role of parents, especially parents of teens, is to give when teens are not necessarily "earning" it. They deserve it because you gave them life and they are yours and special and have something unique to bring to the world. Look how we feel, and we don't even know your teenager! You should feel even more strongly. We believe that your message of love gets through and makes a big difference, whether or not teens show it overtly. Stop reading and go hug your teen!

THERE IS IMPACT ON YOUR TEEN'S SELF-CONCEPT

How children feel about themselves is influenced to a large degree by, if not based on, how they perceive their parents feel about them. If they perceive their parents as critical and rejecting, children are primed, though not condemned, to grow up thinking they are not good enough and that people will not love them as a result. This makes perfect sense. If a parent is treating a child this way, a child can reach one of two conclusions: the parent is unreasonable or unfair or awful, or the parent is correct. Most kids tend to view their parents as "right" even when they do awful things. Obviously, we want our teens to have a good self-concept. Therefore, our relationship with them is of great importance.

LOVE BRINGS SECURITY.
SECURITY BRINGS VENTURESOMENESS.

Teens who have loving and trusting relationships with their parents feel more secure. From that feeling of security comes a greater sense of venturesomeness. We like this word better than *independence*, because we don't believe that teens can or should be truly independent of their parents. But they certainly should *not* be dependent. Then they might never move out! Venturesomeness means that they feel able to go forth and explore, make their mark in the world, and find their own path, but they are still connected. Why are they connected? Because parental love is like a lifeline, it's like oxygen, it's something that strengthens our teens' accomplishments and gives greater meaning to what they are doing.

Venturesome teenagers go forth knowing that it's okay to do so, and that they have their parents' support regardless of exactly what they do and regardless of what their parents actually say. We are not from another planet; we know that parents need to protest weird, dangerous, or highly unproductive things their teens might want to do: "I'm dead set against it!" But we will not stick to those words as often as we might use them. (We will get back to this when we talk about limits.) To do so would be to cut ourselves off from our relationship with our teenagers, something that should be unthinkable to us as parents.

TEENS LEARN THE MEANING OF
LOVING RELATIONSHIPS WITH OTHERS

A strong, positive relationship with their parents also helps teens to internalize appropriate values. Among those values is how to participate in a loving relationship. We are social beings. We need others. Our relationships with our parents help us establish our own sense of self as a worthwhile human being, give us values by which to guide our lives, and help us learn how to be with others and form positive attachments to those outside the family.

This is obviously crucial for establishing intimate, romantic, and family relationships.

LAUGHTER

We mentioned earlier the role that laughter plays in creativity, hope, and optimism. Perhaps the most valuable thing we can say to you is to give you permission to laugh. Laughter is not frivolous. It is not a "waste of time." If love makes the world go 'round, laughter keeps it interesting. We will devote a section in Chapter 4 to ways to make time for family fun and laughter.

But laughter is important in another way. It is a parent's indispensable tool for coping with all the things that teenagers throw at you. As your teenagers try to find themselves, you may need laughter as an alternative to tears or to simply pulling your hair out. "Vintage" garments from the Salvation Army reject pile, jeans worn fourteen inches below the waist, purple or orange hair, black nails, all black clothes, hairstyles that you are unlikely to find in *Vogue* or *GQ*, unauthorized piercings and body art—these and more will challenge you to despair or to keep your sense of humor. To the extent to which we are able to derive pride and joy from things that our teens do, we will be positioning ourselves and our teens for a socially and emotionally healthy relationship.

LIMITS

The word *limits* gets bad press. Teenagers think of limits as restrictions. Parents are better off thinking of limits as "protection," "boundaries," and "guidelines." They are essential for giving our teens focus and some goals toward which to direct their energies. Limit setting is especially difficult today because teens are so aware of others their age who seem to have many more freedoms. Here is one scenario of the kind we hear about quite often:

A boy, fifteen, has friends who seem to be able to stay out as late as they like, use the phone as much as they want, go on-line on the computer without restriction, see R-rated videos and movies, and shop with what seems like an expense account. They seem to have no continuing religious instruction or attendance, or any real responsibilities at home. The fifteen-year-old wants more "freedom" and accuses the parents of being "old-fashioned."

Parents have to listen to their minds and hearts when confronted with these kinds of demands. You may already have concluded that the parents of the friends described are not doing them any favors. But the question remains: How do limits get set? Which ones should we stick to? How do we decide?

If we want our teenagers to grow up to be self-disciplined, responsible, and thoughtful, we must give them opportunities to make choices and deal with limits. It's better to start early in adolescence (actually, earlier than that!), because the issues, such as driving cars, dating, drinking, and going to parties, get tougher and more serious as kids get older.

One of the main reasons parents have difficulty setting limits is that they do not have clear goals for their families, or for their children. When one considers any given opportunity—to go out, to talk on the phone, to be on the computer—it is not hard to say, "What's the big deal?" The big deal is, where does it all lead? What is it doing for our family? For this child? Is the money we are spending being spent wisely, or do we have certain goals that we need to be thinking about when we spend money? Do we want our kids to be well read, in addition to well videoed? Do we care when our kids get exposed to the kinds of violence, language, and sexuality that earns movies their R ratings?

SOME THINGS ARE NONNEGOTIABLE

Parents need to look carefully at the goals they have for themselves and their kids. Some things can and should be what parenting educator and Rabbi Yakov Hilsenrath refers to as *nonnegotiable*. These are areas in which you have the strongest values and feelings and will not change your mind. Of course, as children enter significant new age periods, these things need to come up for review and discussion—like seeing R-rated movies once they turn seventeen or eighteen. Reconsideration is important to show your teens that you have empathy and growing trust for them. But that doesn't mean you are going to change your mind.

Nonnegotiability extends beyond the "thou shalt not"s of family life. It also includes the "You'd better's" (Y.B.). You may feel you want your child to continue religious instruction, do some kind of volunteer or charity activity, take responsibility for certain specific things as part of the home routine, or keep in touch with certain relatives. The best Y.B.s are things that are both important to us *and,* in our opinion, provide an essential life lesson for our children. You may make it clear that these will have to be done before other things—like phone use and shopping— are done. You have every right to teach your child responsibility, and this is a major way of doing so.

Don't Expect Happy Thank-Yous. It is possible, especially if you start early, for them to grasp the logic of what you are doing and to eventually accept some or most of it. But avoid the trap of expecting gleeful compliance. What you want first is compliance; the glee may or may not follow. Be sure to bring up your ideas and values for discussion, at least twice a year. Listen to what your kids have to say when they ask you to modify your position. Question their reasons and listen carefully, using some of the tools we provide in Part 2 of this book. You may find yourself modifying some things, and when this is done in a reasoned discussion, it usually is a positive thing.

Even if you make changes, don't be afraid to bring back an old limit if you feel it is necessary. Just remember not to let your children feel that a limit changed is changed forever.

WHAT ABOUT DISCIPLINE?

We were waiting for this question! It's on the minds of just about all parents. But we will let you in on something we have noticed in recent years. Having written *Emotionally Intelligent Parenting*, we have had the privilege of speaking to groups of parents throughout the United States and the world. We have learned a lot from these meetings, and some of that wisdom we have certainly tried to put into this book, as well as a number of examples. But one thing struck us: Discipline was *not* the main concern of most parents. Most parents were more concerned about how their children will manage in the future, about what kind of human being their child is going to become.

Of course we want the trash taken out and the dishes put away and the clothes hung up, the car brought home when we agree it's coming home, the homework and projects done, siblings cared for when necessary, and curfews respected, and we want to know who our teenagers are hanging out with and where. But the character of our children is something much more than all these, though these are important. And more and more, parents are realizing this.

So, here is our overall message:

Discipline emerges from your overall relationship with your children, the way your home is organized, and the values that you make most visible. Without Love and Laughter, you will have little success with Limits.

DISCIPLINE AND THE ADOLESCENT MIND AND HEART

Let's get right to the most important fact: Teenagers want limits and discipline because these help them feel secure. Discipline, as we noted above, takes commitment, work, and attention by parents. It is a way we communicate our caring to our children. Although most teens would not admit it, freedom can be a scary thing. Teens are faced with frightening choices: Should I be drinking with my friends? Am I ready for sex? What friends do I want? What grades can I get? As we will discuss in the next chapter, these are questions of identity, and a teen's identity is of course linked to what they do and don't do. The latter, despite all the cultural forces at work, still depends a lot on the kinds of limits parents provide and how we provide them.

Very poignant to us is an example of a teenager whose parents were so excited about her learning to drive that they encouraged her to get her license and drive on her own. The parents were, in part, thrilled because they felt driving was a major indicator of passage into semiadulthood and responsibility. Truth be told, they were also relieved to not have to drive their daughter to so many places and to have someone else to send on errands and to pick up the younger siblings.

But the teenager—we'll call her Sheila—was petrified. She was not ready for such responsibility, and like many teenagers who are a little reflective, she realized that her driving training and practice and the demands of the road test did not at all equip her to handle every driving situation. She still wanted someone in the car with her, even though she would bark at her parents' criticisms. In Part 2, we will provide you with some tools for recognizing the mixed messages your teens will often be sending.

The point is, teenagers more than ever need us to provide some limits for them. The world is expecting them to grow up too fast, largely so that they can become independent consumers more quickly, we think. But we can't expect them to ask for limits, at least not directly.

WON'T TEENAGERS RESENT PARENTS WHO ARE TOO STRICT?

Answer: Maybe. Next question, please! Okay, let's stay with this one a little longer. Parents, please take out your union card. You don't know about this? When you are in the hospital giving birth, several largely invisible groups are at work. (Those of you who had home births or elevator births or whatever births will be relieved to know that invisible groups are not restricted to hospitals and were present for you, as well.) These groups, of course, are unions. The two main unions are the PRIDE (Parents' Responsibilities, Ideals, and Dreams Society) and the PURCHASE (Pact Uniting Responsible Children to Harass Adults for Steady [some local chapters substitute *Senseless*] Expenses.

Of the two unions, PURCHASE is far more effective. At birth, children are given a manual outlining different methods of crying to elicit desired reactions by parents. They are taught how to pout and scowl until they get exactly what they want, as well as how to resist tempting offers from parents and other relatives to get them to behave in the adults' best interest. They are instructed in parents' weak points (such as how daughters' tears operate on fathers), and they are given a still-unknown substance that appears to severely reduce or eliminate guilt about asking for toys and other expensive items that, very shortly after purchase, will not be used again.

PRIDE, on the other hand, focuses on the rapture of parenthood, on the wonders and joys of having children…the stuff in all those books you remember reading when you first had children. Notice that except for a very few authors, you rarely see the many writers of those books on the lecture circuit or talk shows—ever wonder why? We will tell you: Most of those books are ghostwritten by PURCHASE operatives.

What's their agenda? They want you to feel incredible love for your children when they are younger and then, when they get to be teenagers, they want parents to want to be…teenagers' best friends. Be their pal, their buddy. Don't upset, deny, or deprive them. Give them more and then more again. Feeling guilty about all that work you are doing, all that life difficulty you may have heaped on them, not being able to provide enough for them? No problem! At least, it's nothing that a platinum credit card, the latest pair of Nikes, or extra time at the mall won't cure.

In the fine print of the PRIDE manual, however, it says something very interesting. It says that you are a *parent*, not a *pal, friend,* or *chum.* You a not a *buddy, crony,* or *peer.* You are Management, not Labor. And with that goes certain responsibilities that take precedence over the goal of being liked. Not that your kids won't like you, or love you, if you provide them with emotionally intelligent limits. They will. But PURCHASE has too many parents believing that Being Liked as a Friend is the overriding value parents should hold. We hope you can now see how this is a subversive plot and not at all true.

Limits support the idea of discipline in that they provide children with a clear sense of right and wrong, even as teens argue and test our word. Actually, the word *discipline* means "to teach," and we need to keep this in mind; our role is not to "punish"; it is to "teach values and skills necessary for our children to succeed in life." What is interesting in contemporary society is the question of a moral source for the limits we set. "Because I said so," which operated pretty effectively in previous generations, does not work well in today's environment, in which teens hear many things from many sources. Some believe that the resurgence of interest in organized religion and spirituality is due in part to a need for parents to have more guidance and backing from "higher authorities." Regardless of the reason, research does suggest that helping our teens find some kind of spiritual connection is valuable to their well-being.

THE IMPORTANCE OF COMMUNICATION

Of course, what we believe can only be inferred by our teenagers from our words and deeds. Therefore, it is important that we communicate to teens clearly and deliberately about our values, family rules, and expectations. And we urge you to take a broad view of this recommendation. We're sure you have seen the advertisements that advise you to talk to your teens about drugs. This is an excellent suggestion, but we need to talk to our teens about everything else as well. In Part 2, we go over communication tools such as dialogue, listening, and working together.

For our teenagers to get our messages, we have to communicate clearly what we mean. We need to give them a chance to understand our point of view. At the very least, they will learn that we *have* a point of view and that we are not parenting by whim. To help them understand that you are doing something they do not like out of love and concern and not because you enjoy restricting them, many parents give teens the "My Job Is to Keep You Safe and Make Sure You Grow Up to Be a Mature Individual" speech.

For those of you who have not done this, or who are dissatis-fied with how it has gone, we provide a model below. The speech, which we present in its full and unabridged form, goes something like this:

PARENT: My job is to keep you safe and make sure you grow up to be a mature individual. When I am sure that you will be safe and can handle yourself in ___ situation in a mature manner, then you can ___ with my blessing.

TEEN: But it isn't fair. You never let me do anything. Everyone else can. You are so ridiculous. Other parents let their kids do these things. And I will be safe. If you never let me do stuff, how can I prove to you that I can handle it?

PARENT: Believe it or not, I do understand how you feel, but you are not allowed to do it, at least not yet.

TEEN: #*&!@#$

The concept of "not yet" comes up often in limit setting and may be a source of disagreement between parents themselves as well as between parents and teens. After all, in most of the areas in which you are providing boundaries and directions, your chil-dren will have to be pretty much self-policing when they move out or go to college. So limits are often about such things as "when" and "how much." One's point of view often depends on one's frame of reference. Many teenagers have as a frame of ref-erence their peers, or at least what their peers tell them, and what they see in the media. Parents, sometimes to a differing degree, take a view more or less informed by emotional intelligence. We look at the whole child, consider his or her growth from child-hood, weigh in recent events, size up what we view as the risks of being wrong in our judgment, and try to take a future-oriented perspective. Teens, being teens, in contrast, tend to be more focused on the here and now. They want your permission to be based on what they did five minutes ago, not last year or even last week.

This is a difficult issue for both parent and teen, but we find it is the cause of greatest difficulty between parents. In addition to the usual give-and-take of views, parents need to be clear as to "where they are coming from" in their opinions. How much of this is based in our own experience, in a traumatic event perhaps? How much is based on what we feel we missed when we were teenagers and want to be sure our kids experience in *their* teens? Most important, how much is based on an appraisal of who our child is, what he or she needs, and what's happening in family and school life right now? Even after these discussions, as honest as they could possibly be, some of our decisions will be inspired guesswork and hunches. And our teens will not hear something convincing from us when we have to explain ourselves.

We urge parents to have limit-setting discussions in private. Get your own act together before talking with your teenagers. We find that it's best to present a united front, although we know some families where something like this is said: "I feel this way and your mother feels that way, and this time we are going along with what she feels."

SELF-MONITORING AND READINESS FOR LIMIT CHANGES

As you can see, setting limits is not a popularity contest, and there are many times when you will agree to disagree. But for a number of issues that involve more logistical than deeply ethical positions, such as when and how homework gets done, bedtimes and curfews, and household responsibilities, it is okay to set up some criteria for teens to prove their readiness for a limit change. After all, limits must eventually be self-imposed and self-monitored, as well as reconsidered on occasion. For those reasons, the skills parents and children possess in goal setting and problem solving help keep teens on course and turn ideas into constructive actions. Within the broad limits we impose, it is valuable to give teenagers some choices. It is not as if our goal is to be restrictive. We have certain directions we want to see our adolescents go in and some areas we definitely want them to avoid. But that leaves quite a lot of room for navigation, and it is valuable to give our adolescents a chance to maneuver. Ways to do this will be discussed under "Contracts" in Part 2. Just remember: Some teens feel especially strong union loyalty and may work diligently to make us miserable for holding them back. However, we are the parents and we have to let go under our terms, not theirs, no matter how much we might sometimes want to just give up.

You might feel frustrated at this point because we are not telling you exactly how to discipline and what this discipline should be. Part 2 will give you some tools to set limits, but we cannot tell you what the rules are for your teens. When and if your teen should drink, smoke, have sex, stay out past 1:00 A.M., or drive with friends in the car is up to you. We have our views, and there are developmental issues that we will discuss in the next chapter, but you have to decide where the lines will be drawn.

These issues have few easy right and wrong answers. For example, how do you feel about your teen drinking a glass of wine with dinner at home? How about as part of a religious ritual? Some argue that this is important to teach responsible drinking. What if there is a family history of alcoholism? How about a sip of champagne on Grandpa's ninetieth birthday? How about a keg party for your teen and his friends at your house so at least you know where they are and can make sure that no one is drinking and driving? Let us clarify one thing about limit setting. While some issues relate to cultural, religious, or personal factors, others involve legal questions. Be aware of what you are deciding by being familiar with the laws about drinking, driving, drugs, and smoking. There are times when we will say to our teens, "We agree with you, but the law is the law."

LINKAGES

Parents, take this test. Go into the bathroom and stand in front of the mirror. (Close the door if you are not alone in the house.)

Look under your shirt and see if there is a large red S there. If there is, then you need not read this section. If it is not there, then you are not Superparent, and therefore might want to read on.

For all the reasons we mentioned in Chapter 1, and many others unique to one's own hectic life, parents cannot reasonably expect to "do it all." Not only that, but we find fewer and fewer parents with the ability to keep up with all that their kids are learning and all the interests and talents they have. It's a networking world, and Love, Laughter, and Limits must be supplemented by Linkages—the vital role of parents to help teens get what they need from wherever they can.

CREATE LINKAGES TO YOUR FAMILY

There are many aspects of linkages, and we will explore some here. To raise children in an emotionally intelligent manner, parents cannot afford to make assumptions. Kids often know far too little about their own families and aspects of their past. (Note that we are clinicians and recognize that some teenagers know far too much about their families and their past. This is one reason why we have come to see the important need for linkages beyond the family, as we will discuss in a moment.) Roots are important. They provide a context in which to understand Limits and also Love. Linkages also can provide sources of Laughter that can supplement what we might be able to generate in our own households. Indeed, one of us has a daughter who rarely lets a meal go by without stating, "You're not funny. Give up. Don't try." Obviously, laughter in that household has to be imported or contracted out.

How to Create Bridges to Family Past and Present. Part of making linkages is building bridges. Here are some excellent connectors we have come across; feel free to add your own:

Music: Generation spanners include Santana; Crosby, Stills, Nash, and Young; Bob Dylan; Jefferson Airplane; Paul Simon;

Billy Joel; swing music, especially some of the originals...but then you had better be prepared to listen to contemporary swing, whether it's Brian Setzer, Big Bad Voodoo Daddy, or the Squirrel Nut Zippers. Remember to give them your recollections about the concerts you attended. Sinatra? I was there....Duke Ellington? Ella Fitzgerald? Front row....Led Zeppelin? Absolutely. It's fun to compare what concerts were like then and now. In fact, some families enjoy having a music festival, where you share some of your songs with your teens and they share a contemporary example with you. Get ready for Limp Bizkit, Shania Twain, Britney Spears, Puff Daddy, and the Backstreet Boys!

Ice Cream: Going out for ice cream (or frozen yogurt or sorbet—we are not barbarians, you know!) or going out to buy some to bring home and eat as a family can be a bridge builder. Talk about where you used to get ice cream. Reflect on the days when strawberry was considered an exotic flavor. Floats and ice-cream sodas are other things we have found some kids are mystified about.

Nick at Nite: Many of us grew up with some great sitcoms that parents and children can watch together; everyone will laugh, and no one will be embarrassed. *Dick Van Dyke, I Love Lucy,* and *Happy Days* are among these classics.

Star ___: *Star Wars, Trek, Next Generation, Deep Space Nine,* even *Voyager* for some can bring many family members together. The videos, the books, the marathons on TV, reruns at all hours, and the music all provide sources of connection...unless you don't believe in the Force.

Great people: Great people span the generations. Among those we have found useful in connecting parents and teens are Bill Cosby, Danny Kaye, Martin Luther King Jr., John F. Kennedy, Billy Crystal, Eleanor Roosevelt, Rosa Parks, Mother Teresa, Twyla Tharpe, and Judith Jamison. Athletes work too: Michael Jordan, Wayne Gretzky, Roberto Clemente, Ted Williams,

Mickey Mantle, Willie Mays, Sammy Sosa, Mark McGwire, Joe DiMaggio, Pele, Troy Aikman, Roger Staubach, Brett Favre, Walter Payton, Florence Griffith-Joyner, and Steffi Graf are just a few of those who might be useful—it's best to find out what a teenager's favorite sports and teams are and to work backward from there. You can also try television and movie characters, such as *The Muppet Show, Sesame Street,* and Disney movie characters.

Comic books: They have changed a lot—get out your old collections and compare notes!

Cartoons and newspaper comics: Whether on radio or television, or in print, some cartoons have changed a lot and others have managed to endure.

Dad's ties and Mom's shoes and hats: There are quite a number of ties, shoes, and hats today that would not have been worn even ten years ago; an opportunity to look at pictures and in other ways compare fashion trends can be a bridge builder.

Old family movies, stories, pictures: Many teenagers get a special charge out of seeing you when you were kids or hearing stories about your childhood.

In hectic times, these moments of linkage remind us, often in emotional ways, of our connections to those members of our household who live with us as well as members who may be departed.

LINKAGES BEYOND THE FAMILY

The Family Context Often Is Not Enough. Linkages are an important way that parents help kids forge the kinds of connections that allow them to develop their talents, make contributions, have a sense of belonging, and build life skills. Our thesis here is that while things that happen in the family context are important, more and more this will not be sufficient for our children's growth. Actually, this is not such a radical statement. School, which occurs outside the family context, is already essential. But we feel that parents (and also schools) must help link our teens with the world, toward making them citizens for the new millennium. As educator Sheldon Berman has said so articulately, our children have social responsibility and must be prepared to be engaged with the world around them. Love, Laughter, Limits, and Linkages combine to fuel children with a sense of appreciation, belonging, competencies, and confidence that will enable them to go forth and make contributions to their family, school, neighborhood, and society.

Linkages and Social Responsibility. Responsibility is the ability of teens to recognize and respond to the needs of others in their family and their larger world. It is an antidote to selfishness, to a me-first or me-always or me-only attitude that some have attributed to many members of our younger generations. We believe that focusing on the "me" issues misplaces the emphasis. We have found that when parents and schools take a visible and sustained role in creating linkages with a world of opportunities and considerations outside their narrow sphere of interest (or self-interest), the vast majority of children respond to this in positive and enthusiastic ways. Kids want to make contributions, as we will discuss in the next chapter. We need to help make this a part of their busy routines.

ARE ALL LINKAGES OKAY?

We tried to avoid this question, but parents keep asking it. There are values issues here, again forcing parents to talk to each other, to reflect on their own upbringing and values, and to generally take advantage of the reflective chances we will give you in Chapter 5.

Certainly, teens benefit from being encouraged to take responsibility for and contribute to their community. This is sometimes welcomed, as adolescents can be very idealistic and grandiose. You want to channel this energy into organizations and causes that are consistent with values that you and your teenager are comfortable with, whether a religious affiliated group, a charity, or a community project. Teens may need some encouragement to do this if their friends are not involved, because it may not be "cool." But we have seen teenagers bring their friends with them.

High schools are increasingly becoming aware of the importance of community-service programs for students' character and social development. If your school does not have such a program, we encourage you to try to get it to start one. Skills for Action (sponsored by the Lions Clubs and Quest International), the Giraffe Program (www.giraffe.org), and Facing History and Ourselves (www.fhao.org) are outstanding, research-supported examples of school-based experiences that help children make important and lasting linkages to their communities and to historical events. Organized programs of volunteering in the community, as well as helping activities of many faith-based youth groups, also provide valuable experiences and opportunities for teens to broaden their life perspectives.

What about connections that mix people of different cultural and religious groups? These are matters that parents will have to think about in detail. For example, we have heard differing views about community and interfaith dances:

"This is a good opportunity for my teen to meet a nice Protestant, Catholic, Jewish, Muslim, Hindu, Buddhist, Baha'i, or atheist boy or girl."

"This is an opportunity for my teen to meet a Protestant, Catholic, Jewish, Muslim, Hindu, Buddhist, Baha'i, or atheist boy or girl."

You read it correctly. The words are almost identical. What differs is the tone of voice! The first one was said with excitement and positive anticipation. The second one was said with dread. We might like the idea of our teenager having friends from different religions or ethnicities, but marrying one of these friends may be, shall we say, a different story. The same may be true of teenagers from different nationalities. Of course, parents' wishes in these matters may not always carry the day. We do, however, have to decide which mixes we want to encourage. What we urge is that these discussions be held first between parents and that our communications to our teenagers be clear and honest.

CONCLUDING THOUGHT

Parents of teenagers lead busy lives, so we want to provide some advice that is relatively clear and practical. Focus on providing your teenagers with Love, Laughter, Limits, and Linkages. Do so in an emotionally intelligent way. In the next chapter, we will review exactly why this is so important for your teenagers, and what it will lead them to develop. In Chapter 4, we will review how to help make your household a place in which these good things are more likely to happen, especially through the use of humor. And Chapter 5 helps you reflect on your life situation and past, so that you can reduce whatever obstacles might get in the way of your carrying out these ideas. Parts 2 and 3 will give you a tool kit to use as you carry out our suggestions, and lots of examples of how to use the tools in a wide range of parenting situations.

Chapter 3

What Our Teenagers Require for Healthy Identity Development

Things are different today, I hear every mother say...

—THE ROLLING STONES

The times they are a-changing.

—BOB DYLAN

What was your adolescence like? Sex, drugs, and rock 'n' roll, or studying, athletics, and the classics? Perhaps some combination? Regardless, things are different today. The world has gotten more dangerous on a personal level. We don't spend time worrying about the Bomb anymore, but we do worry about our kids' classmate with the attitude who was just disciplined by the teacher. And parents of teenagers carry around with them a dread about HIV and AIDS.

The world of our teenagers today also is filled with paradoxes. Are schools violent or are they really safer? Should we be worried about drugs or not? There seem to be more areas than ever where our teenagers could use some guidance, but they don't seem eager to allow us into their world. We have the global community of the Internet, where teens will chat with strangers about their most intimate thoughts (anonymously, of course) while often keeping from their parents such simple facts as where they are going or what they are doing.

And our teenagers, who may seem to have it better than we can ever imagine, certainly better than the previous generation, are balls of stress ready to bounce off the walls. A 1999 Brandeis University study of teens aged thirteen to eighteen found that virtually all of them reported being under a lot of stress. When does the stress let up? Studies of parenthood do not suggest that this is a time of life for great relaxation. Maybe when we become senior citizens? What do we do while we are waiting?

The pace of life and the realities of greater danger combine to create continuous new challenges for today's parents of adolescents. To meet those challenges in an emotionally intelligent way, we need to understand our teenagers' goals, their concerns, and their search for identity. We will discuss this below; then we will review what Love, Laughter, Limits, and Linkages "do" for our adolescents that is so important. We will close with a little "ages and stages" information for you. In the spirit of respect for the realities of our lives as parents, we are not going to be complete; we are going to focus on the areas that we have found matter the most.

FINDING A POSITIVE, CONSTRUCTIVE IDENTITY: THE FOREMOST TASK OF ADOLESCENCE

CHALLENGES THAT TEENAGERS FACE

Virtually every teenager is walking around looking for answers to these questions about himself or herself:

How can I understand who I am now and who I will be in the future?

How can I nurture and build positive relationships?

How can I develop skills to handle everyday challenges, problems, decisions, choices?

How can I develop to be a moral, ethical, active, committed human being?

How can I develop a positive, constructive identity?

Teenagers don't actually verbalize these things often, if at all, and sometimes what they are doing seems almost opposite to a search for the answers to some of these questions. Nevertheless, if parents start to understand teens' behavior as revolving around these questions, we are less likely to assume that our issues of the past are their issues in the present. Our job as parents is not to *give* them answers to these questions—no parent can do this successfully. Our job is to help them *find* answers, and to guide them toward opportunities and relationships and skills that will allow them to develop sound answers.

Erik Erikson, a pioneer in focusing on identity as the main developmental task faced by adolescents, warns us that adolescence is a process, not an end product or even a stop along the highway of life. There are about as many pathways to accomplish this as there are families. Yet these pathways are part of one large road map. The route to a positive, constructive identity passes through certain checkpoints:

• Trust: During a child's early infancy, parents' responsiveness to their needs leads children to feel a sense of trust and worth that cannot adequately be put into words. Indeed, it is not a verbal phenomenon for infants; it is visceral and emotional. When children are not given adequate care, they emerge from their infancy with an equally hard to describe sense of mistrust in the world.

• Autonomy: Toddlers start toddling and parents start worrying—where are they going, what are they getting into, are they safe? But this toddling has an important place in identity development. It allows children to develop a sense of autonomy, the feeling that they can go and do certain things sort of on their own. We say "sort of" because kids need to stay in touch with their "home base." Knowing that parents, loved ones, and their home are safe and available to them gives them the courage to venture forth without worrying, as many of our early explorers did, that they might fall off the end of the earth. Obviously, without a sense of trust, developing autonomy is difficult and becomes quite limited, accompanied by strong doses of shame and doubt.

• Initiative: The elementary school years are a time for initiative taking. That means starting a lot of things without necessarily finishing them, or without caring about or truly understanding what it means to finish what one starts. This often upsets parents and teachers, who, as adults, place greater value on closure. But it's the job of kids to continue to try to explore possibilities. What a wonderful building block for identity it is when children emerge from this period of life with a strong sense that there are lots of things that interest them, that they have tried many things and that lots of them were positive, worthwhile, fun, rewarding. What we don't want to do is burden our kids with guilt for trying and not completing. That is an example of where focusing on *our* agenda at the expense of what our children need can set the stages for later difficulty.

• Industry: This is Erikson's term for the ability to do something in detail, in depth, with great persistence, almost to the exclusion of anything else. In the preteen years, maybe even into early adolescence, we find children who seem obsessed with Power Rangers, Cabbage Patch dolls, or the fad at the time of our writing, Pokémon. As each of these phenomena bursts onto the scene, there is a frenzy and urgency that leads one to think it will never subside. But they all eventually do. Meanwhile, children are given an opportunity to become industrious about collecting, trading, learning everything possible about a subject, finding rare items, and so on. This is the same kind of thing we see with baseball and other trading cards, comics, series of books, watching every episode of the "hot" television shows, and the like.

IDENTITY DEVELOPMENT INVOLVES ZIGGING AND ZAGGING

So, parents, please keep in mind that development works in a kind of zigzag way. First, the kids trust you, then they seem to want to get away from you. But after that zag is a zig...they become attached securely, which allows them to go forth in confidence and come back to "safety." Then they are off starting all kinds of things without finishing them, only to get incredibly focused and almost obsessive about one or two things. But again, there is another zig—they come back to earth and learn how to start and complete a number of different things.

Identity is the next stage, occurring in adolescence. It is accompanied by a host of physiological, cognitive, and life-circumstance changes that make this such a challenging period of time. We are not going to discuss these in detail; we reviewed them in *Emotionally Intelligent Parenting,* and there are books on "ages and stages" of adolescence, such as the *Boys' and Girls' Books About What Is Happening to My Body,* that do a fine job with such information. We want to emphasize three things:

1. Cognitive changes lead adolescents to begin thinking abstractly, more about what might be and could be, rather than what is. Thinking about and envisioning the future is not so foreign for them anymore. They feel more and more comfortable speculating and wondering. As they wonder, their emotions are more closely connected than ever to their thoughts. When a young kid tells you she wants to be a basketball player, she is not really thinking deeply about what that means and especially not about the likelihood of failure. Even if you tell her she probably won't be able to, she might be upset, but it will not last long. For teenagers, the interplay of thinking about the future and strong emotions about the future is powerful. What they might or might not be starts to matter a great deal...so much so that many teenagers go to great lengths to avoid thinking about it and having to deal with the strong emotions that will be invoked.

2. As a result of these processes, you can expect to see some extremes of emotion and thinking. This is part of the process of zigging and zagging until kids get their course relatively straight. You will see hypersensitivity of emotions, especially in response to criticism. ("I can't believe she said that to me! That #!@$&!" "What did she say?" "She said my skirt was cute." "What nerve!") You will see catastrophizing, so that only the worst possible outcome of any situation is anticipated. ("I will never pass that test, not in one million years, no matter how much I study." "Do you

think it would help if you opened your book?" "No, because even if I got a great grade, he would still not give me anything more than a B because he hates me so much." "How do you know that?" "Are you kidding? I just know.") And you will see exaggeration. ("That was the most amazing concert I have ever, ever seen in my whole life." "How many has it been? I've lost count." "This is my second one. Everybody from school is planning to go to the next one, right before Thanksgiving. We will all miss school." "Who is getting the tickets?" "I'm not sure." "Maybe we can arrange a car pool. How about if I get in touch with Lillian and Tali and Miriam's parents and see who will drive?" "I don't think they can go." "Oh. Don't you have some things to take care of for tomorrow?" "No. I mean, yes, I've gotta go.")

3. The opinions of teens' peers start to matter a great deal. But don't think for one second that your influence is any less important. And all the hypersensitivity of emotion and exaggeration apply to what you say and do...especially to the negative things, but certainly also the positive. You are the steering wheel for their journey. They might run off the road, their wheels might become misaligned (we will talk about the wheels shortly), or there might be other mechanical problems. You must keep your eyes on the road and never let go of the wheel. Just because they don't seem to be listening or they quote their pals Shirley or Tommy as if they were quoting Scripture does not mean that they will ignore the values you emphasize. But, as we noted earlier, it is harder and harder for our messages to come through all the competition unless we are clear and consistent.

LOVE, LAUGHTER, LIMITS, AND LINKAGES HELP WITH IDENTITY

Now, let's also be realistic. It is not easy to have a positive impact on your adolescents, especially if you do not already have a great relationship with them. There really are just few things that parents can do, consistently, that can make a very big difference in preparing adolescents for competence in adulthood. Realistic simplification is the strategy of choice. There is only so much that parents can do, are willing to do, and can keep track of.

That's why we focus on Love, Laughter, Limits, and Linkages. It is through parents' creative combination of these concepts that teenagers can come to see that they are worthwhile, cared about, blessed with certain strengths and skills, and connected realistically to the world so that they can put their skills to use in ways that are going to lead to appreciation and contribution.

WHAT TEENS NEED ON THE ROAD THROUGH ADOLESCENCE: A, B, AND THREE C'S

If we think of adolescence as a journey or a passage between leaving childhood and emerging into adulthood, then all along the journey adolescents are considering their experiences against a backdrop of questions related to their emerging sense of identity: "Who am I?" and "What can I become?" The road is quite congested, the routes are not clearly marked, and there are dead ends and detours galore. How do parents guide their teens without jumping behind the wheel and taking over, especially at signs of trouble?

Parents don't exactly have the dual controls that driving instructors do. Parents have to provide some kind of guidance to help teens move along in their journey in a positive way, as well as fuel to keep their kids going strongly. (If this is starting to sound a bit like a computer game, well, just remember where you saw it first!)

In the spirit of simplification, we believe that Love, Laughter, Limits, and Linkages serve many purposes. One of them is to make sure that the wheels of the vehicle are all in place, on tightly, and in alignment and balance. These are the wheels that are going to take our teenagers as far as they are going to go. They are the A, B, and three C's we mentioned earlier:

APPRECIATION

What are your teenagers' cherished talents? Maybe you see this in their hobbies. Maybe you don't see it because it happens in the privacy of their rooms or only with trusted friends. Be alert to what it is your child really likes and seems good at. It might be math, science, languages, writing, computers, creative media, art, music, getting along with other people, sports, dance, outdoor activities, sailing—the list is endless. Howard Gardner refers to the "multiple intelligences" as the range of talents that children have, and he explains that their future identities are strengthened when they have positive outlets to express and develop these talents. Giving your teens a chance to discover and develop their talents is a bit tricky and sometimes leads to a dead end, but these efforts can make a life-changing difference.

These talents become a centerpiece for helping your teenager feel appreciated. Certainly, this is an outcome of our showing them love and sharing laughter. The sense of appreciation, of celebration, is an essential part of our teens' lives. It is something they need in order to venture out into the world and try out identities with confidence. Our home must be the place where accomplishments are given appreciation.

BELONGING

Teens need groups to belong to. That's what motivates some to join gangs. They are looking for places where they have a role or a purpose, somewhere to find positive peer relationships and be with others who have similar interests or abilities. They need places to learn things, where they can have inspiring leadership and feel safe, comfortable, and accepted. Sounds like an ideal extended family, doesn't it? Well, in this era, this describes too few families. But clubs, teams, youth groups, and community organizations can serve this purpose. Through building bridges and creating linkages, we help our teens have that sense of belonging that tells them, in part, who they are and perhaps who they want to become. Remember, though: The best groups are those that provide the sense of community and identity that teens are looking for, although some advertise this but do not deliver.

COMPETENCIES AND CONFIDENCE

Many will wonder, What about independence and autonomy? Isn't that what adolescence is all about? Perhaps at one time it was. But we live in an interdependent world. There is no such thing, in any practical sense, as independence and autonomy. And as parents, we don't want our teenagers living lives independent from us and our families! We like our kids! That's not to say that they should be dependent. We must avoid, in the new millennium, tendencies to think only in opposites, or in terms of either-or.

We live lives of synergy and interdependence. Our children need competencies to allow them to deal with a range of possible opportunities. These include the skills of emotional intelligence, to have the balance of smart and heart that one really needs to manage effectively and sensitively in the world today. Parents need to look for opportunities that will allow kids to learn:

- how to recognize and label their feelings and those of others;
- how to manage their own strong feelings, often so that they can carry out essential responsibilities;
- how to set goals and plan, both long- and short-term;
- how to work in groups as team players and as leaders;
- how to build positive relationships with many different kinds of people;
- how to be a thoughtful problem solver and decision maker; and
- how to bounce back from roadblocks that one faces.

Our teenagers develop these competencies from the combination of Love, Laughter, Limits, and Linkages in their lives. Many skills are developed out of the need to accomplish tasks related to limits and linkages. As competencies develop, confidence follows. And confidence allows teenagers to try new areas of possible identity, to take positive risks, to stretch themselves, to expand their competencies. When these efforts are surrounded by love and supportive laughter, setbacks are not devastating. Catastrophizing is temporary, as their strengths are continuously held up for them to see.

On page 61, we include a chart with a more detailed discussion of competencies of youths in middle and high school and we outline some ways that parents, as well as schools, can work together to foster growth.

CONTRIBUTIONS

Parents, this is the area. This is the wheel to pay special attention to. This is the one that our hectic, consumer-oriented society keeps throwing nails at. In reality, feeling a sense of contribution, selflessness, and generosity is essential for healthy identity development in teenagers. We hear a lot about teens' tendency toward being self-centered, but that is really because the teen years are so much about self-discovery. It is not about selfishness—unless we allow it to go in that direction. Teens thrive on helping, on making contributions to causes, saving the environment, assisting senior citizens, teaching what they know to younger or needier kids, working in soup kitchens, supporting political campaigns, raising funds for people who are suffering, helping their religious institutions reach their charitable goals. Making contributions and feeling like a contributing member of groups to which we belong and care about are key parts of what makes for a well-balanced, caring person. And teenagers are motivated to develop their competencies in the service of making contributions. Now you can see why we felt it essential to add Linkages to Love, Laughter, and Limits as guiding approaches for emotionally intelligent parenting of teenagers.

Because contributions are so important to our adolescents, we want to focus on several areas to which you can particularly attend.

Contributions to the Household. We are busy, and our kids are busy; they don't seem to have enough time for their schoolwork, special projects, and sleep. How can we add to their burdens? You do them no favors when you shield them from their responsibilities. Part of their responsibilities are to make contributions to your household. Everyone has to, and our children are not exceptions. Indeed, the earlier you start, the easier it is, though for some teenagers, it would not be easier even if you started in utero.

Part of your task is a matter of framing. First, you must believe that making contributions is essential for the growth of your child and that linkages to the household are a way of accomplishing this. Second, you must reframe the odious arena of "chores" into something a little more uplifting. Few of us like to do "chores." Chores are a chore. We hire others to do our chores whenever possible. However, we like to make a "contribution." Contributions make us feel good about what we are doing and about ourselves. Contributions are a way of giving, of showing love. When put in these terms, it may be easier for the teen to accept and may also be easier for the parent to expect. Remember, without opportunities to make contributions to the family, teens are being denied a chance to grow both in that area and in learning responsibility.

Contributions to One's School and Community. Marian Wright Edelman, child advocate and educator, has been known to say, "Service is the rent each of us pays for living." There is much to contemplate in these wise words. How does this get put into action? In *Promoting Social and Emotional Learning: Guidelines for Educators* (published in 1997 by the Association for Supervision and Curriculum Development), members of the Collaborative to Advance Social and Emotional Learning (www.CASEL.org) reported on a visit to LaSalle High School in Providence, Rhode Island. At LaSalle, any student who wanted to be a member of a sports team, varsity or intramural, had to develop and sign a contract that stated three goals in each of three areas: How will you improve yourself in your sport? How will you improve your team? How will you improve your school or community?

CASEL has found that the schools can play an important role in fostering a sense of contribution through service. But families also have a role to play because of the power of parental modeling. Many families do take seriously their responsibilities for charitable giving. But we must look at exactly how this happens and what we are communicating to our teens. If we write and mail checks with little or no comment, we are missing an opportunity to make a linkage and help our teens (as well as younger children) develop a sense of contribution. Here are ways to increase the meaningfulness of our giving:

1. Talk to your children about the array of causes competing for your dollars. Talk about what they do and why you (and they) think the work is important. At times, this might involve research, which the Internet will make easier than ever. Decide as a family to whom you will contribute and why.

2. Consider having your children join you in making contributions. They can add some money to causes you all agree to, or they might have groups or organizations they feel they want to support.

3. Personalize your service-related work as much as possible. Our children's sense of perspective and empathy as well as their own feelings of contribution are enhanced as they get more personally involved in the service work. Take them with you when you do volunteer work. Let them be as directly involved as possible. As they spend time in these situations, which are very different from their own experiences on the surface, they are more and more likely to feel the sense of contribution, in addition to understanding it intellectually.

A report put out in 1997 by the Council of Chief State School Officers, on behalf of themselves and the Association for Supervision and Curriculum Development, the Character Education Partnership, the Close Up Foundation, Earth Force, and the National Society for Experiential Education, puts into clear perspective the reason why contributions are essential for our adolescents:

> If we are honest, the deepest reason we educate our children is not just to equip them with the knowledge and skills they will need to achieve economic success and personal satisfactions. We do it to get them in touch with their own humanity. We want them to see themselves in others' eyes, and to feel others as a part of themselves. We want them to stand for something, and to be able to act on the basis of the kind of person they understand themselves to be. We want them to understand that the ills of the world belong to the whole community, that the problems that may be someone else's fault are not always someone else's job. We want them to understand that we all belong to one another.

The Spirituality Connection. We don't often think about the linkage of adolescent identity and spirituality, but there is more and more agreement that we cannot ignore this connection. A fundamental premise of spirituality is that each of us is important to the world. By extension, our specialness means that we have contributions to make, and spirituality is part of our ability to make deep connections to whatever it is that we believe gives life meaning.

Of course, adolescents do not often recognize what they are experiencing as an awakening of their spirituality. Rather, they are more in touch with beginning to struggle to find meaning and purpose in life. Their cognitive abilities allow them to ask questions about the future, and their moral reasoning moves them toward perceiving that there are overriding values, as well as many more gray areas than they saw in their preteen years. Adolescents are entering a search that will continue throughout their lives, as they author their identity through their deeds.

Adolescence is a time for important questions to emerge... we mean, beyond what time does the mall open and can I have the keys to the car. Parker Palmer and Rachael Kessler, who shared their insights in a 1999 special issue of *Educational Leadership* devoted to spirituality, have spent a great deal of time with adolescents; these are among the most frequent questions they have heard:

- How does my life have meaning and purpose?
- What gifts do I have that the world wants and needs?
- To what or whom do I feel most deeply connected?
- How can I rise above my fears and doubts?
- How do I deal with the suffering of my family, my friends, others in the world, myself?
- What or who is it that awakens or touches the spirit within me?

Each of these "big questions"—about purpose, gifts, connection, fears, suffering, and personal spirit—all take on added meaning when a religious context is added to secular considerations. But a spiritual connection is important with or without any involvement in religion.

How do parents guide adolescents in the spiritual area? The most powerful tool we have is modeling. By that, we are referring to how one lives one's own life, rather than specific principles we try to get our children to follow. It relates to how we go about making contributions and putting our lives into perspective. Many parents find that creating linkages is the best strategy. Adolescents have a hard time putting into words their beliefs about "transcendent" ideas. It is often easier for them to begin by relating to real or fictional stories of others' experiences. And these kinds of discussions may be carried out effectively in youth groups.

We have seen many benefits resulting from guiding adolescents to reflect on matters of the spirit. It has provided valuable perspective and ignited a sense of contribution that is rich, deep, and meaningful. The more adolescents are able to reflect on the kinds of questions noted above, with adult guidance and peer support, the more in touch with their own spirituality they will be.

CONCLUDING THOUGHTS

A parent's main task is to provide opportunities, not to be the source of all learning. In our complex and hectic society, parents must also maintain a balance among various possibilities and responsibilities, avoid teen overcommitment, and try to find the best alternatives for their particular teens among the many available. And we must do this while knowing that we can't make all the decisions for our teens; sometimes they will not have the best experiences. Here our role is to be empathic, not to say "I told you so!", and to help them reflect on what happened and what they can learn from it.

Nevertheless, we must also recognize that life events can be quite disruptive and challenging to the developmental flow. Certain "Developmental Derailers" tend to occur at different periods in adolescence:

• Middle School/Junior High School: Becoming a big brother or big sister to a sibling; dealing with family moves; coping with divorce; dealing with death in the family; dealing with a classmate's drug use or delinquent behavior

• High School: Coping with divorce; dealing with death in the family; changes in parental job situation; dealing with a classmate's drug use, delinquent behavior, injury, or death due to violence, pregnancy, suicide, HIV, or AIDS

There is overlap between the lists, and these are just guidelines, of course. In all of these instances, our best advice to parents is to continue to provide Love, Laughter, Limits, and Linkages toward helping your teenagers feel a sense of Appreciation, Belonging, Competencies and Confidence, and Contribution. Indeed, the A, B, and three C's will get thrown into doubt when the derailers take place. Teenagers' identities are not so secure that they cannot be shaken by disruptive crises. As parents, our task is to keep the vehicle of development on the road, with all wheels moving.

And what is the fuel that parents need to provide or to see that their teens get? Inspiration, imagination, joy, optimism, humor, caring, support, firmness, safety, clear values, and, perhaps most important, respect. Because they are teens, they will experience intense emotions along the journey, especially in difficult times. With our support, those emotions will neither hold them back nor misdirect them. Then teen aspirations can soar into adult accomplishment.

A PRACTICAL OVERVIEW OF KEY AREAS OF ADOLESCENT DEVELOPMENT

Earlier, we took a look at the way in which identity is developed through the teenage years. Let's take a closer look at some of the major areas of growth in youths of middle and high school age.

Middle School/Junior High School
The Big Picture
There are two areas that we find most prominent:
- Being aware of sexual factors, recognizing and accepting body changes, recognizing and resisting inappropriate sexual behaviors
- Developing skills for analyzing stressful social situations, identifying feelings and goals, carrying out request and refusal skills

Key Competencies and Areas for Confidence Building

Feelings
- Self-aware and self-critical
- Harmonizing of one's own conflicting feelings

Thoughts and Attitudes

- Recognizing the importance of alcohol and drug abuse and prevention
- Establishing norms for health
- Setting realistic short-term goals
- Seeing both sides of issues, disputes, arguments
- Comparing abilities to others, self, or normative standards; abilities considered in light of others' reactions
- Acknowledging the importance of self-statements and self-rewards

Actions

- Initiating own activities
- Emerging leadership skills

What Works Best with the School: What Can We Ask of Schools and Help to Ensure They Do

- Respect teens' need for physical outlets (minimize the sitting/lecturing mode of teaching)
- Give outlets for creativity (e.g., vary types of student products, deemphasize written reports)
- Give opportunities to participate in setting rules
- Provide very clear expectations about truancy, substance use, and violent behavior and be sure they know them
- Give opportunities for setting and reviewing personal norms and standards, meeting academic goals
- Encourage membership in school-related groups, academic, athletic, or otherwise, as well as those linked to, but outside of, school

Belonging

Peer Issues

- Talk to teens about choosing friends
- Help them develop peer leadership (versus followership) skills
- Help them deal with conflict among friends
- Clearly show that you recognize and encourage alternatives to aggression and violence
- Recognize that belonging and being included are very important

Family Issues
- Be prepared for conflict between your values and peers' values in areas such as clothing, music, importance of and time devoted to schoolwork
- Share with and teach them about stages in adults' and parents' lives
- Encourage rituals, even after formal "rites of passage" might occur; don't let the glitz overtake the meaning; passages *must* include appreciation, belonging, competencies and confidence, and contributions, as well as fun

Particular Areas for Appreciation and Contribution
- The workings of democracy, government, press, and media
- Importance of the environment (Spaceship Earth; earth as habitat, ecological environment; global interdependence; ecosystems)
- Prejudice, freedom, citizenship, and liberty
- Understanding and accepting differences in one's community
- Identifying and resisting negative group influences
- Developing involvements in community projects
- Apprenticing of and training for leadership roles

High School

The Big Picture

By the high school years, our concern should be less with teaching "small" skills and more on how teens integrate the skills they possess. The best arena for teaching new skills is when teenagers recognize they are needed to accomplish something that *they* want to accomplish. Here are the areas where teens need skills to move ahead with confidence; we will follow this with a list of competencies you might want to focus on developing in your teens if they have difficulties in the confidence areas.

Areas for Confidence and Accomplishment
- Maintaining positive relationships with peers, adults, authority figures, maybe even parents
- Being healthy—diet, nutrition, energy levels, sleep, skin care, dental care, personal hygiene, physical exercise/sport/dance
- Becoming a knowledgeable, responsible, nonviolent, caring citizen—contributing to community service or environmental projects, understanding elements of government and participating in them

- Dealing with love and loss—with peers, in family
- Functioning with emotional intelligence in a workplace
- Earning and budgeting money
- Planning a career and preparing for an adult role
- Developing personal goals, interests—hobbies, clubs, future education plans
- Meeting responsibilities
- Finding outlets for ideas, creativity, inventiveness
- Encountering and nurturing one's spirituality

Competencies to Be Alert To

- Listening and oral communication
- Competence in reading, writing, and computation
- Learning to learn skills
- Skills in personal management: time management, prioritization, self-organization, goal setting, planning, self-monitoring
- Genuine personal and moral evaluations of self, actions, behaviors
- Recognizing consequences of risky behaviors (sexual activity, drug use), protecting self from negative consequences
- Harmonizing of own and others' feelings
- Adaptability: creative thinking and problem solving, especially in response to barriers or obstacles
- Feeling pride in work accomplished

What Works Best with the School: What We Can Ask of Schools and Help to Ensure They Do

- Encourage recognition of personal strengths
- Help teens to make realistic academic plans
- Encourage and teach persistence in achieving goals in spite of setbacks
- Plan career or post–high school pathways
- Give opportunities, help in building effective group participation: interpersonal skills, negotiation, teamwork
- Help teens find avenues for making a contribution to classroom or school (e.g., school or community service or volunteer work, being a role model for younger students, helping senior citizens, homeless, poor, other needy individuals)

<u>Belonging</u>

Peer Issues
- Effective behavior in peer groups
- Peer leadership and responsible membership
- Using request and refusal skills
- Initiating and maintaining cross-gender friendships and romantic relationships
- Understanding responsible behavior at social events
- Dealing with drinking and driving

Family Issues
- Maintaining a level of mutual interdependence, autonomy, and connectedness
- Talking with parents about daily activities, learning self-disclosure skills
- Preparing for parenting, family responsibilities

Chapter 4

Making Your Household
an Expanding Oasis of Peace
in a Desert of Pressure and Stress

Are you ready to take the Neighbor Test? Here it is: Imagine that you and your children are having an argument with a little testiness...with some harsh words...okay, okay, with lots of screaming. A neighbor comes to the door—what happens? "Oh, hello! So glad to see you! Come on in. We are all civil here. Isn't that so?" "Yes, we children are even more civil than our parents. We are as civil as can be..."

Chances are, everyone will stop fighting. And the longer the neighbor stays, the less likely you all are to pick up where you left off. What does this mean? It means that while it's very hard to avoid being angry, family members—starting with parents, who must serve as role models—can usually limit the hurtful expression of their anger.

Think again of the neighbor at the door: What if the person stayed for an entire day? We would somehow manage to keep to ourselves lots of things we might want to say. Many of these things would be hurtful expressions of our own stress and upset and not helpful for our children to hear. It is unlikely that they will complain, "I missed your telling me how irresponsible I am." Or, "My day is not complete unless you threaten to ground me."

No, they will not miss those extra parental words. Parents, make an agreement that you are going to go an entire day without saying the kinds of things to your teenager (you can do this with all your children) that you would not say if a neighbor were there. Don't worry about your children getting the wrong message from this. Try to do it for one full day, and keep track of how close you come. Can you make it to 4:00 P.M.? 6:00 P.M.? 8:00 P.M.? Whatever you can do is great; then try again until you can manage it for an entire day.

You are very likely to find that you feel better at the end of the day and that your teenager is a little more positive and receptive to you. You probably wouldn't do this all the time, but you might want to bring it into your household routine once a week, or so. It's not as easy as you think, but the results might surprise you!

TEENS NEED PLACES TO FEEL COMFORTABLE

The Neighbor Test is just one aspect of making our home into an oasis of peace amid a desert of pressure and stress. It is so important that teenagers feel their home is a place they can return to in a positive way. The world of school and peers can contain a lot of put-downs and reminders of inadequacies. Where are teens going to go to feel comfortable? Many of them transform their rooms into a private place, a fortress, a moated castle against the stress of life. We find this quite understandable. Remember, the developmental process teenagers are going through leads to cognitive exaggerations. Among these is the belief that everyone can see all of their faults. Their rooms become rare safe havens, "lead shielded" from prying beams from the outside world.

What else can parents do besides the Neighbor Test to make their homes a bit more appealing, maybe even so comfortable that teenagers will venture outside their rooms a little more? Some of the bridge-building ideas we mentioned earlier can help. And so can these.

HOW TO START THE DAY WITH A WARM, POSITIVE GREETING FOR YOUR TEENAGER

Think about how you wake up your teenager. What is our first greeting like? Is it sort of military? ("Okay, time to get up. Lots of things to do. Fifteen minutes to shower. Twenty-three minutes for breakfast. Bus at 0700 hours.") Is it kind of businesslike? ("Wake up. You have clothes to put away, homework to finish, and you need to put out the garbage before you have breakfast.") Might it be, dare we say it, psychological? ("Wake-up time! How many times do I have to tell you? What's wrong with you? Why can't you get up in the morning? Why do I have to nag you over and over again? You are so much like your uncle.")

Try something a little different. Think of yourself as a greeter, an usher, someone whose job it is to get your teen launched into the day with good spirits, to get cooperation as the morning "performance" unfolds. When you do this, and do it consistently, you will find that it has a role in reducing household tension. Here's how to greet:

• Use your child's name and the word *good* or its equivalents in a short sentence. If possible, use an ethnic greeting or a greeting from another language your teenagers might be studying ("Good morning, Tom!" "Hi, Tammy, it's a great day today!" *"Boker tov,* Tali! Looks like a fine day today!" *"Bonjour, bonjour, Theodore...comment va tu? Très bien, j'espère!"*)

• Don't dwell on frustrations, shortcomings, difficulties, or the like that might be on *your* mind related to your child but are *not* likely to be his or her first wake-up thoughts. Save it for later and keep neutral if that's the best you can do. ("The weather is just terrific, the leaves are turning color, what a day!" "It's hot as all get-out today. I think we are talking shorts for sure." "I don't know about you, but I had some weird night's sleep. Dreams I can hardly remember. Glad I'm awake." "Another day, another room full of molecules. I can almost see them bouncing around and circling one another." "Would you like a sports update or are you going to try to catch CNN/SI before you leave?")

• Don't roll your eyes or make other nonverbal cues of disbelief at the response or lack of response to your greeting. Do *not* expect your teenager to bounce out of bed with gusto. Do *not* expect deep conversation. Above all, do *not* expect appreciation for being awakened. What you are doing is providing a nonneg-ative start to the day. The power of being greeted is recognized in many cultures, and it certainly is known in the retail business. But it doesn't always lead to a sale. Sometimes, all you are doing is defusing an emotional brain ready to function in attack or rejection mode. You are giving it little to fight with. Sometimes your kids might attack by reflex. You must not roll your eyes, mutter, or divert from your positive path if you hear one of these responses:

"Will you get out of here?"
"Shorts, are you nuts?"
"@$)#($&@! the leaves—who cares?"
"Leave me alone."
"Take your molecules and go bother somebody else."

Ah, the joys of parenting! This is *not* a time to say, "Don't talk to me like that," although we all know that such talk is already forming on most lips. It's *not* a time to say, "You see, I try to be nice, and this is what I get! That's it! I'm fed up!" And we recom-mend against something supportive like, "Listen, mister, I'm not the housekeeper here. Get your rear end out of bed in five min-utes or else you're going to get it." Personally, we are always intrigued with what the "it" is that kids are going to "get."

No, this is a time for strategic retreat. We recommend that you become a timekeeper and a consultant: "Let's see...my watch has six forty-five and your clock has six-fifty. Close enough. You can have lots of time for breakfast and whatever else you need to fin-ish up, or you can take a little longer. I'll be downstairs if you need me for anything."

• Leave positive messages on their answering machines, send positive E-mails, leave encouraging notes. When they reach for their clothing, they might encounter a Post-it note saying, "I'm proud of you," or "You really worked hard and prepared well." At breakfast, there might be a note that wishes them a good morn-ing or a good day or good luck on an upcoming exam or the like.

An E-mail waiting for them when they get home after a tryout or a tough class also helps.

Will they thank you? Don't count on it. But they will appreciate the positive attention, and they will be aware that they are feeling something other than the usual pressure.

BRING HUMOR AND A LIGHTER TOUCH INTO YOUR HOUSEHOLD

Humor reduces anger. Households in which humor has a strong and regular place find anger is expressed less harshly and less often. Humor also reduces stress and increases our tolerance for one another. It helps to create a climate that teenagers find "okay" to be in. The alternatives—stress, pressure, disputes—are what too many families experience too often. We are confident that you are "with us" and are ready for some ideas to bring humor, or at least a lighter touch, into your household.

INCREASE YOUR HOUSEHOLD H.Q. (HUMOR QUOTIENT)

• Cut off **cartoon captions** and write your own. This can be a fun family activity. A related fun game is Mad Libs, where everyone creates a story by providing words representing certain parts of speech in a fill-in-the-blanks format. Mad Libs are available in most book and card stores.

• Have a **humor corner** in your house or classroom. Pictures, books, Internet jokes, silly poems, crazy ads, and whatever else people find funny would go there.

• Have a **laugh break**. This can really help at homework time, especially when kids are stuck. Short tapes or segments of audio-tapes or videotapes or time to read from humorous books or cartoons can really make a huge difference in a situation that can bring out a lot of anger. It is hard, frustrating, and ineffective to just sit there and "keep trying" when one is truly stuck. Humor is energizing, encourages creativity, and puts us in an optimistic frame of mind. This is exactly what kids need to bring with them when they are working on a homework assignment. We find that eighteen to thirty minutes (sometimes less for some teens) of frustration working on an assignment that one is not "getting" is the point of diminishing returns. That's when humor breaks are especially valuable.

PARENTAL REFLECTIONS

Patty Wooten, R.N., has a Web site called Jest for the Health of It at http://www.JestHealth.com. This phenomenal source for family humor offers ways to create a lighter, more positive mood. In their home's humor corner, parents might want to post some of these observations from her Web site, both for their own continuing sense of perspective and to give teenagers something to think about:

- A child will not spill on a dirty floor.
- A youth becomes a man when the marks he wants to leave on the world have nothing to do with tires.
- An unbreakable toy is useful for breaking other toys.
- Avenge yourself; live long enough to be a problem to your children.
- Be nice to your kids, for it is they who will choose your nursing home.
- For adult education, nothing beats children.
- If a child looks like his father, that's heredity; if he looks like a neighbor, that's environment.
- If you have trouble getting your children's attention, just sit down and look comfortable.
- Insanity is inherited; you get it from your kids.
- It rarely occurs to teenagers that the day will come when they'll know as little as their parents.
- Money isn't everything, but it sure keeps the kids in touch.
- Never lend your car to anyone to whom you have given birth.

- You can learn many things from children...like how much patience you have.
- Summer vacation is a time when parents realize that teachers are grossly underpaid.
- The first sign of maturity is the discovery that the volume knob also turns to the left.
- There would be fewer problems with children if they had to chop wood to keep the television set going.
- The best thing to spend on your children is time.

ADVICE TO TEENAGERS WHO WRITE THEIR OWN ABSENCE EXCUSE NOTES, AUTHORIZED OR NOT

If you want to start your teenagers off (or maybe set them off), you might want to share this bit of practical wisdom: Always have someone carefully edit and proofread all forged notes you send into the school. Here is a list circulated as coming from schools in New Mexico, apparently written by teenagers who wanted to fake their absence on a given day:

1. Dear School: Please excuse John from being absent on Jan. 28, 29, 30, 31, 32, and also 33.

2. Please excuse Dianne from being absent yesterday. She was in bed with gramps.

3. Chris will not be in school because he has an acre in his side.

4. John has been absent because he had two teeth taken off his face.

5. Lillie was absent from school yesterday because she had a going over.

6. My son is under the doctor's care and should not take fizical ed. Please execute him.

7. Carlos was absent yesterday because he was playing football. He was hit in the growing part.

8. Please excuse Joyce from P.E. for a few days. Yesterday she fell off a tree and misplaced her hip.

9. Please excuse Ray Friday from school. He has very loose vowels.

10. Please excuse Blanche from jim today. She is administrating.

11. George was absent yesterday because he had a stomach.

12. Ralph was absent yesterday because he had a sore trout.

13. Please excuse Rita for being absent. She was sick and I had her shot.

14. Please excuse Lupe. She is having problems with her ovals.

AND NOW A WORD FROM THE WORLD OF SCIENCE: ARE YOUR TEENS OKAY? DOES YOUR TEEN HAVE ESPN DISORDER: EMPATHIC SPORTS PSYCHOLOGICAL NEED WITH DEPRESSION/ELATION SUBTYPES?

We feel it is our duty to alert you to the latest happenings in our field, especially those related to the ever more popular world of sports. Mental-health professionals are reporting a new illness that strikes a number of adolescents, Empathic Sports Psychological Need disorder, usually referred to by its technical label, ESPN. The most severe outbreak of this condition has been in the New York area, but a number of cases have been reported in Cleveland, Boston, and as far west as Arizona. Centers for Disease Control (CDC) officials have not formally commented, but off the record they have indicated that they doubt that the ailment was introduced by such unknown foreign agents as a bioweapon.

There are apparently two strains of this affliction, ESPN-Depression and ESPN-Elation. Not surprisingly, ESPN-Depression appears to be more widespread. There are some indications, from the Boston area in particular, that this is a chronic ailment. Among its more interesting features in the Boston manifestations is something akin to a thought disorder. Recent clinical observations revealed that a subset of Bostonians afflicted with ESPN-D believe in something called the Curse of the Bambino. Apparently, some supernatural force is operating on a certain region in Boston in and around Fenway Park, as well as in sports venues occupied by the Boston Red Sox at key professional moments. Chief research associate psychologists (CRAP, for short) from the Psychic Network have suggested that these spirits must be inhabiting team transportation facilities. This will get all the follow-up it deserves.

You may have noticed some of these signs of ESPN-D or ESPN-E in your teenager:

Despondence following losses by their favorite team

Mumbling and muttering about umpires

Quick recycling of the newspaper

Watching PBS voluntarily

Cutting out sports pictures in newspapers and magazines before parents read the paper (could be a symptom of either subtype)

Demand for sports haberdashery

Euphoric smile despite your asking about homework

Mimicking of broadcaster phrases ("Oh baby!" "Holy cow!" "It is high, it is far, it is...gone!" "At the wall, looking up, see ya" "Yes, and it counts!" "Stick save and a beauty." "Here comes a one-timer from the circle." "That was some hit—*boom.*" "My homework's done, myyyyyyyyyy homework's done!")

Some corroboration was found in a recent case study in which an afflicted Red Sox rooter repeatedly invoked "Comma, Comma—it's got to change!" After searching lexicon databases, researchers determined that the invocation was not an insult to broadcasters' or Yankees' grammar, but rather a plea for a change in "Karma," yet another spiritual allusion.

During each major sports play-off season, the CDC suggests that the nation's mental-health professionals enter a state of red alert. ESPN disorders of epidemic proportions are likely to be observed in October in such cities as New York and Atlanta. A June outbreak is likely in Los Angeles, San Antonio, Portland, and Miami. And there is a bulletin out for St. Louis, where years of underlying ESPN-D have been reported, now replaced by a robust outbreak of ESPN-E traced to one Kurt Warner. By the same token, a disaster-relief team is being sent to San Francisco, where ESPN-D of magnitude 8.4 has been reported. But one weekend can turn much of that around. Stay ready, parents! ESPN disorders can strike anywhere, anytime.

FAMILY GAMES:
THE MIDDLE SCHOOL VALUES SHUFFLE

We find that some families look forward to playing a game once each week. These can be board games, word games, card games, even computer games. Some families like to get out of the house and throw around a Frisbee, play tetherball, or try other outdoor games. What matters most is that competition is on the back burner and fun is on the front burner.

More and more parents seem interested in games that focus on family values. These can be tricky to introduce with teens. Your best chance is usually early adolescence. Here is a generic type of homemade game you can use or create variations from. If it is played in a spirit of humor, it actually can work quite well.

Make a deck of twelve index cards, each one labeled with a value—for example, Family, Peace, Knowledge, Popularity, Wealth, Good Looks, Good Health and Long Life, Friendship, Patience, Fame, Acts of Kindness, Do Your Own Thing. There should be a deck for each member of your family. There are a number of variations you can play and invent. Here are some:

• Give everyone a deck and ask them to separate the cards into two piles, more important and less important. Then divide each of those piles into two piles, more important and less important. Share the top and bottom piles, at least.
• Pair up. (If you have an odd number, two people can work as one "team.") Each person in the pair has two decks of cards. Order the cards in terms of their importance for you, with the most important on top. Then take another deck and order the

cards in terms of how important you think your *partner* feels the values are, again with the most important on top. Take turns uncovering one card at a time, comparing what you predicted with what your partner actually feels, and vice versa. You will learn how well your opinion of your family members' values matches what they themselves think. This will give you insight into your family and, most important, of course, your teenager.

• Take two decks and shuffle them; there will be twenty-four cards in total. Deal out all the cards to members of the family. Each person takes, from among the cards they hold, the one card that represents the least important value to the family and places it facedown in the middle. Then everyone passes one other card to the person on their right. Once again, each person winnows out the card with what they believe is the lowest value to the family. Keep passing and discarding until each person has only one card left. This card will represent a value highly regarded by the family. Now each person takes a turn putting their card faceup and saying why they think that particular value is important to the family; or they can give an example of a time when the value was put into action. Sometimes the luck of the draw leads an important value to have been left out. Someone will mention it, to be sure. Once you have your final list, consider posting the cards on the refrigerator and reviewing them from time to time, especially when the family is in turmoil.

GUIDING QUOTES

More and more, parents need some grounding and guiding inspiration. At a workshop we did where we presented this idea, a woman came up to us afterward and showed us a yellowed piece of paper that her mother had given her when she was a teenager. It had a quote on it from John Cheever about love being the most eternal form of success. She told us that she often looked at it for guidance. Since that time, we have asked for other parents to think of quotes they can use to help ground them and guide them, as well as quotes they might like to give to their children for them to carry around. Try it…you will find that it is a way to convey goals and values without being heavy-handed. Here are a few quotes that some parents have used for guidance and/or given to their children for inspiration:

"Most people are about as happy as they make up their minds to be."—ABRAHAM LINCOLN

"If you can walk, you can dance. If you can talk, you can sing."—ZIMBABWE SAYING

"You are not required to finish the work, but you are not permitted to stop working."—ETHICS OF THE FATHERS

"We can do no great things—only small things with great love."—MOTHER TERESA

"Nothing can bring you peace but yourself."—RALPH WALDO EMERSON

"I have a dream…"—MARTIN LUTHER KING

"Ask not what your mother can do for you, ask what you can do for your mother."—VARIATION ON JOHN F. KENNEDY'S FAMOUS INAUGURAL ADDRESS

"I cannot and will not cut my conscience to fit this year's fashions."—LILLIAN HELLMAN

"Remember, no one can make you feel inferior without your consent."—ELEANOR ROOSEVELT

"There is more hunger for love and appreciation in this world than for bread."—MOTHER TERESA

GUIDING JOKES

In the same way that some people collect quotes, others collect jokes. Actually, it's a question of what "speaks" to you, what gives you a sense of perspective, a chance to step back, to take a break from everyday stress and pressure and look at the world in a different way.

Jokes can be especially valuable for that, because so much humor is about looking at the world—and our children, and our relationships—in a new way. One of our favorite jokesters is

Dr. Ed Dunkelblau, past president of the American Association of Therapeutic Humor and a consultant to businesses and parent groups on how to bring humor into everyday life.

Ed helps people take a new perspective on rejection—a common issue for teens—by telling them humorous stories that open up new ways of thinking:

Did you hear the story of Fred and his talking dog? After many rejections, they land a job as part of a show—a big breakthrough. They get on the stage and Fred asks, "What does sandpaper feel like?" and the dog says, "Ruff." "What is on top of a house?" Fred asks. "Roof," the dog answers. Fred then asks, "Who is the greatest baseball player?" "Ruth," says the dog. With every answer, the crowd reacts more and more negatively, until finally they call Fred and his dog impostors and throw them both out on the street. After they brush themselves off, the dog looks up at Fred and says, "Do you think I should have said Mickey Mantle?"

This story is a good one for teens who think the "crowd" is always right and who are afraid to be innovative. It allows one to have faith in one's talents, yet be sensitive to the need to show it in ways that can be seen and appreciated by others. It capitalizes on the emotional, physiological, and perspective-broadening aspects of humor.

Another story is based on the reversal of expected roles. It is a valuable motivating tool for teens who think they are on a negative life track:

A bus driver and a deeply religious man die on the same day. They are brought before the heavenly tribunal, and the bus driver is immediately admitted to heaven. The religious man is told to wait while his case is examined more carefully. Outraged, he protests, "I am a pious man. I taught many classes. And I know for a fact that the bus driver was not at all religious." "That is all quite true," says the heavenly angel. "But when you taught your classes you caused many people to sleep. When that driver drove his bus, everybody prayed."

Start generating your own quotes, jokes, and stories!

HANDLING EVERYDAY REMINDERS WITH HUMOR

This is a polite and politically correct way of saying that parents need to find a better way to nag than the ones they are using now. Teens are tired of the old routines. They have their parents' reminder and nagging strategies and approaches memorized and can probably do a fabulous imitation of you. We certainly have seen some good ones over the years!

In *Emotionally Intelligent Parenting*, we introduced alternative ways to get kids to do things around the house and to meet their responsibilities better. We based this on emerging communications technologies that we suspect children like better than nagging. We have upgraded our examples for teenagers:

An answering-machine message from an undone assignment:

"Hey, wassup? The name is English, English Paper. You remember me? We were hanging out for a while together but then, I don't know, it's like, you were hanging out with your friends, which is cool but, hey, I, ya know, need to get done and here I am, like, waiting in the bottom of your locker or something, I really don't know where I am. I've been talking to this guy, I think his name is Shakespeare, and he says like, 'To be or not to be,' and I really want to, like, 'be.' I know you say you're gonna get to me, that I am on your list and I should just chill. But, hey, this has to happen for me, so, if you could, like, please check me out soon."

An E-mail from a science assignment:

<Warning. A computer virus has been circulating that affects unfinished science assignments. This virus causes the assignment to remain unfinished, thus causing damage to grades and possibly college admission. It is not clear how the virus works. Some say that it stimulates the Laziness Lobe of the brain; others say it attacks the Sleepiness Area. In addition to backing up all software, it is recommended that assignments be completed

ASAP. If this is not done, other assignments can also be infected. In the most severe cases, the individual affected loses the ability to drive and is unable to hold electronic equipment. Unfortunately, there is no known fix for this other than assignment completion. Please pass this warning to your friends.>
J. William Gates

A handwritten note from what were once called "chores" and are now called "contributions," waiting to be completed:

> *Yo!*
> *Do you see me sitting in the sink?*
> *I'm getting crusty and I'll start to stink.*
> *My friends are caked up, very thick with goo.*
> *And over there the bowls are starting to stew.*
> *The things in the fork are starting to fuse,*
> *Your keys to the car, you're about to lose.*
> *My grammar may be lousy, but I'm here to say*
> *You better clean the dishes before you go away.*
> *No 'scuses you be trying, ain't gonna take no crap.*
> *No matter what you say, you just won't beat this rap.*

PREPARING FOR THE ANTIHUMOR, ANTIFUN ATTACK!

Parents, be prepared. As you launch into a humor corner or in other ways begin the process of bringing more humor into the household, you might find yourself under attack. Oh, if you only could invoke the Neighbor Test in reverse! But we promised you realism, and so we want to prepare you for that attack by sharing a related kind of attack on one of us.

This was a direct assault on the brain, or on the lack thereof. For we suspect that, like one of us, a number of parents may not have brains. This was discovered via the following scenario and subsequently confirmed by others of the same ilk:

DAD: I see you have an English assignment left to do and a test to study for tomorrow.

SAMARA: Yeah. I'm gonna take a break now.

DAD: You've been working for fifteen minutes! What kind of break?

SAMARA: *Dawson's* on [referring to *Dawson's Creek* or any other teen show of the moment] and I have to watch it.

DAD: Hold on. We have a VCR for just this purpose. Tape it tonight and get your studying done and you can watch it tomorrow.

SAMARA: No way! *Everyone* in the high school is watching tonight and *everyone* will be talking about it first thing in the morning. You must have no brain if you think I'm going to tape it and watch it tomorrow.

All dads and moms who have found themselves biologically brainless yet still in need of some kind of brain for everyday use are encouraged to copy the picture on page 82 and carry it around with them.

Actually, the picture can be quite helpful. Notice the white central area. Most teens will agree that parents possess this part of the brain—the brain stem, which controls functions like ambulation, elimination, and respiration.

More doubtful is whether you have the next, shaded area, known as the "emotional brain." This is kind of interesting. The emotional brain controls our response to threat, our fight-or-flight reactions. It's the place where we register all those feelings of helplessness as our teenagers talk circles around us and, through sleight of hand that any magician would envy, make our money disappear.

In fact, for those of you missing this part of the brain, we provide, in our final chapter, a guide to your and your teenagers' emotional states. Of course, not all of us were able to do this from direct experience....For now, it's helpful to keep looking at the brain and to remember that our teenagers have the same brain structure as we do, though they might not want to admit it!

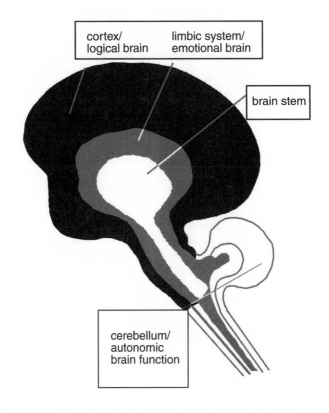

The outer area of the brain, the largest and the most recent to develop, is the thinking part of the brain, and its job, among other things, is to make sure that the emotional brain does not react too quickly, too often, too extremely, or too harshly to what is going on around it. Over the centuries, we have had less and less need to react to life-threatening physical danger on an hourly basis (although this is not as true as any of us would like it to be in certain circumstances—during war time, in conditions of extreme poverty, and in violent neighborhoods, for example, as well as in certain kinds of jobs). We now find that our emotional brains are more regularly attuned to threats to one's sense of self, to identity. So we have an emotional brain designed to be quick to spot threats and move us to react in ways to minimize those threats. We have a thinking brain designed to look at things more carefully, from different angles, and see if we really need to react quite that dramatically to a threat or if perhaps the situation does not pose a threat at all.

Enter the teenager! As we have discussed, teenagers are working on establishing a sense of identity, of who they are. As these different aspects of identity are being tried on, Filene's-like, over a period of days and weeks and months, the teen has many opportunities to perceive threats to these emerging definitions of self. The thinking brain really has to work overtime, which can certainly relegate to the back seat concerns about schoolwork, household responsibilities, cleaning one's room, extended family members, and the like.

It is not wrong to point out that parents, even those of us with little brain content, are going through similar issues. While our children are becoming teenagers, some of us are entering stages of our lives where we start questioning who we are and where we are going in life. Yes, this is an identity issue, and this means that our emotional brains are also working hard to protect our sense of self. Oh, the torture to our sense of self-image when we notice that, as young as we think we are, we don't appear to look quite as youthful as our teenagers and their friends. Their definition of skin and hair, when they are at their healthiest, makes our Oil of Olayed and Rogained versions of those human attributes a bit shaky. But let us not be a source of offense and worry to you. Please feel free to disagree with us and think you are as wonderfully youthful and amazing as your emotional brain and thinking brain can conspire to allow you to believe!

Regardless, once you're armed with the brain we have provided and a bit of perspective, we hope you can withstand the assault on your selfhood that may accompany your attempts to raise the H.Q. (Humor Quotient) in your household. Naturally, the more you can involve your teenagers in setting things up, choosing games, adding to the humor or quotes corner, and the like, the greater will be your chance of success.

BACK TO THE NEIGHBOR TEST

What happens when we run into difficulty with the Neighbor Test? On the surface, some people think it looks so easy to do. But, as we said earlier, it's quite a challenge. And as you try to make your household a more peaceful place, your initial attempts may bring forth reactions that would make Barney turn purple and Emily Post as pale as can be. Well, maybe just more purple and more pale, respectively.

Parents we have worked with have identified their top five strategies for hanging in there during the Neighbor Test and then minimizing the negatives that result from making an unneighborly comment before the end of the day:

- Control your initial reaction: Ask yourself, "Is this really something to be angry about?" "Would I want a neighbor to hear this?"
- Control your initial response: "What can I say or do that will be most helpful now?"
- Control your reaction to another's response to your anger. If your anger has led to an angry response, which is typical, your next choice is: "How can I keep this from getting worse and worse?" "What would the neighbor say?"
- Control of your next reactions: "How can I bring some calmness to what is happening?"
- Apologizing for what you said or did: When anger does occur, it's still useful to let your children know that things may have been done or said in anger that were not meant. The alternative is to let your children think you *did* mean what happened!

ROAD SIGNS FOR PARENTING YOUR TEENAGER

We conclude this chapter with another way of helping you get a new perspective on your parenting and a way to keep your cool and use the 24-Karat Golden Rule.

We think of parenting as a journey, and certainly a lot of parenting is spent in the car, driving our kids places, driving as a family, and, eventually, teaching our teens how to drive. Rabbi Eliot Malomet first helped us see the analogy of road signs to everyday parenting issues, and *Emotionally Intelligent Parenting* has a series of comparisons that he inspired. But his kids are very young, and we found a whole new set of road signs that speak to us as parents of adolescents. Along with the signs, we provide some Emotionally Intelligent Parenting travel tips for responding in a AAA way.

LANE ENDS—MERGE AHEAD

This sign gives parents a positive way of knowing for sure that we are entering a new stage in working with our children. Whatever road we were on before is now changing. There are some warning signs; however, we don't always pay close attention to them, and sooner or later we reach the sign that says Lane Ends—Merge Ahead. We must be ready to make the changes necessary to parent a teenager and not a preadolescent. We are not being architects of the road to be traveled. As noted earlier, there are developmental pathways that teenagers will follow, and that's the road that lies before us. As we prepare to merge, we must be ready to look at this new road for what it is, and not assume that it is simply another version of the road we have just left.

So, parents, be on the lookout for those early signs that the road is merging. Prepare yourself! Recognize that Love, Laughter, Limits, Linkages are going to be the focus of your parenting for the upcoming teenage years.

DEER CROSSING

We chose Deer Crossing, as opposed to any other animal crossing, because in our more optimistic moments we like to celebrate the exuberance and joy of adolescence. That's what the Deer Crossing road sign symbolizes for us. Above all, adolescence is a time of great enthusiasm. It may come at a time in our adult lives when the idea of leaping and prancing is replaced by sitting and watching. Nevertheless, we must celebrate and encourage our adolescents' useful enthusiasm. Adolescence is a time of great idealism. Our children will become involved with social causes. They will look upon lessons that they learned earlier about hunger, poverty, and injustice, and one or more of these ideas is likely to ignite in our teenagers a concern, an outrage, and a commitment to action. This we need to encourage.

But youthful enthusiasm is not limited to social causes. Our teenagers are likely to get excited over television programs, new fashions, hit records, and social triumphs large and small by their friends. In fact, be prepared for the range of emotions in your household to increase dramatically once you have a card-carrying teenager in your abode. Just like deer, excited teenagers do not always pay close attention to speeding cars. So we, as the experienced drivers, must be on the alert and help channel some of the enthusiastic spring of our deer so that they keep out of harm's way. It is always a bit of a challenge to not be the wet blanket, to not be the one that says this is impossible, that can't be done, you are wasting your time, and other such distinctly adult remarks. We would not have liked our own youthful enthusiasm to be sandbagged in that way, and our kids don't like it, either. Listen, encourage, and use as your guide the concept of the Hippocratic Oath: avoid harm. By that we mean that we should be alert to when our youths' enthusiasm might lead them into harm, but we should be less concerned about shielding them from all discomfort, unpleasantness, or difficulty.

FALLING-ROCK ZONE

When we drive along the highway and see this sign, we cannot help but look up at the cliffs next to us and wonder if this is going to be the day that we finally get to see a boulder or maybe even just a rock fall in the falling-rock zone. For parents of teenagers, the road they are traveling has similar thrills. We know that some risky things can take place. We just don't know if and when they are going to happen to our teenagers. So as we drive, we look up at the rocks and wonder. In some zones, there are various forms of protection to keep the rocks from getting onto the main part of the roadway. We can liken these to social supports available in our schools, families, and communities. But no amount of social support, like no amount of netting or fencing, can provide a guarantee that some rocks will not fall, or that they won't cause serious damage. We must accept this as part of nature and not spend all of our waking hours looking up at the rocks waiting for one to fall. The reality is that the rocks don't fall frequently and the truly harmful rocks fall very, very rarely. Also true is that we need to be more in touch with our teenagers than we typically are, given our hectic lives, so that we might notice when the rocks are starting to loosen. For indeed, rocks rarely jump from a secure, spontaneous place on the cliff down into the middle of the highway. There is a process of loosening, and when it comes to our attention, we can get the rock technicians to help cement the rocks into a safe place.

But things do happen; we are not as vigilant as we might like to be; there are occasional jolts in the earth that send rocks flying that had previously seemed secure. At those times, we must be prepared to stop what we are doing and clear the road. We must devote our energies at those times, which may be times of drug use, eating disorder, depression, or even severe withdrawal from everyday life. We must be prepared to shift into a new gear to change our driving patterns, to abandon whatever journey we thought we were on and get that rock securely back on the cliff, where it naturally belongs.

FOG ZONE

More common than falling rocks is fog. Here, the fog zone has two aspects. First of all, it denotes times when our youths appear to be confused, unsure of where they are headed—in short, in a fog. But our focus here is on you, and you probably spend more time in more dense fog than your teenagers do. Part of the problem is that we keep thinking that the fog has some direction, some purpose, some meaning, when it is simply fog. Fog is a state of confusion where we cannot see what's around us. At those times, it is best to proceed with caution, to not make highly decisive moves, and to be patient. One thing about fog is that it comes and it also goes. The time to move most quickly is not when we are in a fog. The time to get the greatest illumination from our headlights is not when we are in a fog. Often, it's a time to pull over to the side and wait, or to proceed very, very slowly. In these complex and hectic times in which we are parenting our teenagers, we will indeed find many moments of confusion and uncertainty. We will not be able to see fifty feet ahead of us, although we will feel we should be able to. These realities must be respected. Natural forces, such as fog, are the result of a combination of climatic conditions and ground properties and do not arise through magic. If we think of fog as having the adaptive purpose of slowing us down, providing a little extra moisture, and then clearing up when it is wise to proceed, we can feel less pressured about trying to remove the fog and can simply increase our vigilance.

TRAFFIC CIRCLE

We have so many associations with this road sign that we do not know where to begin. Traffic circles are reminders that the teenage years are indeed times when our children get behind the wheel of thousands of pounds of fast-moving metal and use these devices to propel themselves to various eating and shopping establishments. We are not sure of many more difficult "normal" moments in teenage parenting. Fresh indeed are the feelings of trepidation at being in the passenger seat without the dual controls that the driving instructor has. But this is in so many ways an excellent analogy for being a parent of a teenager. We are indeed with them, but we do not have the controls we had when we were driving and they were in the infant seat or strapped into the seat alongside us. Our lives are, literally and figuratively, much more in their hands.

And in this stressful situation, our teenagers will encounter traffic circles. Traffic circles are traffic engineers' ways of providing I.Q. and E.Q. tests at high speed. One would think there would have been better ways to guide the flow of traffic than some of the traffic circles that we, living in New Jersey, have seen. Nevertheless, the traffic circle means that our teenagers face many choices and must make these choices while people around them are driving along at breakneck speeds; some of these other drivers on the road know where they are going, and some do not. Teenagers have little way of telling the difference. At any moment, one of these drivers can change course very abruptly and cut off our teenager. When do we signal, when do we merge, how soon to get into that left lane. What do I do if I miss that turn?

These are the concerns that our teenagers face, and there is no blueprint we can give them for the answers. They will learn as they go through many traffic circles. What we can do is to encourage them to talk about their experiences, to reflect upon what they have done and why they did it. Perhaps we can offer some useful advice, helping them look toward the future. Advice of the kind that begins, "You should have..." earns "technical merit" points but not "style" points.

Our teenagers need future guidance, and so when we speak with them about the errors of the past, we must do so in a way that sustains their confidence and helps them believe that they can—and indeed have better skills to—handle the future traffic circles they will encounter. Very sad to us are circumstances in which teenagers avoid traffic circles because they feel they can't handle them and/or because they already hear their parents' admonitions after they have made a mistake. Teenagers are quite subject to our criticism (a topic we address explicitly later in one of our sound parenting bites), and so we must always be conscious of whether our comments are designed to help them master future difficulties or "frighten" them into being highly cautious and avoid situations that cause *us* worry and angst.

REST STOP AHEAD

Parents, drop the battle here! Put down your shields! Sheathe your swords! Get off the parenting road, be a road warrior no longer, and go to a rest stop. Parents of teenagers need to take breaks. And our teenagers need us to take breaks. So let's pull into these rest stops and avail ourselves of the facilities they have to offer. And what are those? There is gourmet food. There is boutique shopping. There are the elegant rest-room and washing facilities. There is all the beauty of nature that one could ask for.

You are reading in disbelief? You are wondering what kinds of roads we have in New Jersey? You know about the New Jersey Turnpike. Everybody does. Perhaps we are referring to the Garden State Parkway. No, we are not. We have simply entered the altered mind stage that comes upon parents of teenagers more often than we would like to admit. At those times, we must use our strength of mind and imagination to take a psychic break from parenting our teenagers.

How can we take this kind of break? One way to practice is by beginning to look at rest stops that we come to on the highway as if they were owned and operated by Donald Trump, Steve Wynne, or Michael Eisner. This will require that we not think about what's right there in front of us. We must be willing to put aside our ongoing worries, concerns, therapy sessions, tutoring endeavors, and the like and give ourselves a rest. We need to recharge our batteries. If we cannot find it possible to leave our teenager somewhat on his or her own, then we must make alternate arrangements for our teens, as well as any other children we happen to have, and get some time for ourselves as parents. We need the "pause that refreshes." Much as we will discuss teens doing homework, in all human endeavors one reaches a point of diminishing returns, where our energies and creativity are no match for what the moment requires. At those times we need to regroup, recharge, rethink, reengage our own sense of fun, wonder, and possibility, and then come back, ready to be creative, to be attentive, and to provide a high level of Love, Laughter, Limits, and Linkages.

NARROW BRIDGE

"The world is a narrow bridge, but the most important thing is that we are not afraid." This saying, from the collected works of Rabbi Moharan, is very important parenting wisdom for those of us with teenagers. It means that the road in front of us will, at times, become very narrow. We will wonder if we can pass through it. We will find ourselves pressed to the limit of our endurance, our resources, our abilities, our time, our emotions. But the most important thing is to not be afraid.

Many, many others have traveled down the road of parenting teenagers. The bridge has been designed for us to pass through, and if our vehicle is a standard-sized vehicle, then we are likely to be able to proceed. Love, Laughter, Limits, and Linkages are our guardrails and our guides.

Some of us, however, are not carrying standard parenting loads. We may have one or more children with special physical or emotional needs. We may find ourselves scraping against the sides of the bridge. It may indeed be too narrow for us, though fine for most others. At those times, parents need to find an alternate route, a different path. But in doing so, we must not be afraid.

Parents must proceed with confidence because it is confidence that our teenagers need from us. The teenage years are limited in number, and our children are rapidly heading toward adulthood. We want, and need, them to arrive at adulthood with the experiences and abilities they'll need to manage in the future. We want them to have opportunities for Appreciation, Belonging, Competencies and Confidence, and Contributions. With these as part of their vehicle, our teenagers can take the wheel and drive through the world's narrow bridges to find their way onto the roadways of adult life with confidence, and not with fear.

Chapter 5

Don't Start with Our Teens,
Start with Ourselves
The E.Q. Parenting Survey

Take a look at yourself and make the change.

—MICHAEL JACKSON

Where did you learn to parent? It's not something we think about a lot. But when it comes time to start dealing with teenagers, it's a good idea to at least take a look at the influences on our parenting, as well as the resources that can help us. There are four major areas we'll want to explore:

1. Our history, how our parents parented us, will help us see how we learned to parent for better and/or for worse.

2. Where we are in our life, what our context is, will impact on how we feel today and how we parent (and actually on how we do everything else, too).

3. We need to understand our emotional reactions, especially how our teens can push our buttons, so that we can improve the way we handle these troublesome situations.

4. It is also essential that we know our strengths, because we are going to need them. We like to look at things from a strengths perspective rather than a deficit model. We find that people are more motivated when encouraged to use their strengths than when criticized for their weaknesses. (Hint: This also applies to our teens.)

Are you fed up yet with all of this self-reflecting and self-awareness? It's a lot of work and a real pain in the neck or heart or someplace. Why can't we just be oblivious of our own thoughts and tendencies and patterns? Everyone else seems to be oblivious. The cliché is "Ignorance is bliss," not "Reflective self-knowledge is bliss." So why open this Pandora's box of self-awareness? Why look at oneself? Doesn't another cliché say, "What you don't know won't hurt you"?

Well, we are finding out that some clichés are quite wrong. For example, "Sticks and stones may break my bones, but names will never hurt me" is one *n* away from the truth: The "never" should be "ever." And it is also the case that what we don't know about ourselves can hurt our teen. Most of us can't afford to parent blindly by instinct, because instincts are tied to aspects of our own upbringing that may or may not be applicable to current situations with our children. As we will say often, it's important to parent by choice and not by chance.

We find parenting surveys helpful in giving parents insight (we thought we would try another word for self-awareness) into influences on parenting. We start with parenting history because, for better or for worse, how we were parented impacts on how we parent. We need to look at our parents as role models and teachers. We learned most of what we know about parenting from them. For some of us, this is a frightening thought. For others, it can be reassuring. For others still, who knows what to think?

We also look at the past because the present is so much different. Our parents' generation had their challenges, such as the Great Depression, World War II, the Cold War, and the 1960s, but raising a child today is quite scary and difficult. Today's adolescents are faced with influences that we never had. Sure, we had to contend with sex, drugs, and rock 'n' roll when we were growing up, but not the same way as kids do now. Teens today have easier access to these things in a culture that supports their use and during a time of less adult supervision and more media influence. We find parents are often more hesitant to say no because we don't want to be negative, we want to be our kids'"friends," or because we, too, experienced these things and survived and don't want to be hypocritical...or interrogated.

Next we need to look at where we are in life, what our life circumstances are. Who is placing demands on us? What is expected of us? For many of us, feeling overwhelmed is all too familiar. The age of technology and globalization has just meant that we have to do more, and do it quicker and cheaper. Business competition has forced a demand for greater productivity at all levels. Our children have also fallen prey to this harried and driven lifestyle: extracurricular activities, grade pressures, SAT preparation courses, and after-school jobs. We often do not have the time for ourselves and for each other that would enable us to refuel emotionally and learn the values of the family.

It's ironic that when we are emotionally close to people, we are more easily "emotionally hijacked" by them. Where our children are concerned, we can get hijacked if we see ourselves in them and see something we strongly like or dislike. In either case, they can exploit this in us for their own ends.

One important task for adolescents is to separate from their parents and forge an independent identity. (To "forge" an identity is the usual and appropriate cliché, because it connotes a lot of heat and banging.) For example, it is a lot easier to rationalize disobeying someone we are angry at; when our teens get angry at us, it can support their justification for doing something we don't want them to do because we are so "mean," "stupid," "old-fashioned," "overprotective," or just plain "nuts." It may seem sometimes that no one can annoy us more or make us angrier than our teenagers. We need to be aware of our feelings regarding our teens so that we can react to them in a more helpful manner. At times it is almost impossible to avoid getting angry with our kids (and probably unhealthy, as well), but we want to react in a way that will help get our messages across.

Finally, we are going to need to look at our strengths, which we will need during trying times, but we also want to lead with our strengths in general. A lot of books like this one can make us feel like total failures and inadequate parents. This helps nothing.

We have to be aware of and draw on our parenting strengths to help our children. We need to keep our strengths in mind at all times.

THE E.Q. PARENTING SURVEY: KNOW THYSELF

Your Parenting Past

Complete the following survey exploring your relationship with your parents. Place an X over the number for how you felt about your parents during adolescence and circle the number for how you feel now. Use one color for your father, another for your mother, and others for any additional parenting figures.

a. Closeness:

Very close						Not at all close
1	2	3	4	5	6	7

b. Honesty:

Complete openness						No communication
1	2	3	4	5	6	7

c. Emotional support:

Supportive						Uninvolved
1	2	3	4	5	6	7

d. Financial support:

When necessary						None/dependent
1	2	3	4	5	6	7

e. Contact frequency:

Comfortable						None/too much
1	2	3	4	5	6	7

f. Approval:

Unconditional acceptance						Critical
1	2	3	4	5	6	7

g. Approach to discipline:

Fair						Harsh/overly lenient
1	2	3	4	5	6	7

h. Other aspect of parenting: _____

1	2	3	4	5	6	7

There are many ways to look at our relationships with our parents. We did not want to make a survey the size of a telephone book. We provided a blank line so you can add something important to you—for example, was your time together fun or not fun; would you say their response to changes or difficult situations was flexible or rigid? Use these ratings as a way to reflect on your past and present relationships with your parents. What is the overall trend you observe? Is it pretty good or not so good? Does it improve or deteriorate over time or at different points in time? How do your parents differ from each other, and how do your relationships with each one differ?

Now go back over the above scale and use it to *rate yourself in your current relationship with your teen.* Cover your old ratings and rerate, or just put a square around the number that applies to your teenagers. You might even find that you have different ratings for each of your children. What do you notice? Are you just like your parents in some ways? Are you like one of them more than the other? How are you different?

Most important, what areas would you like to change? Are there ways you feel you want to shift your ratings in your relationships with your teens? In this book, we are not going to tell you how to feel and how to think. We want you to decide that. But the key word is *decide;* we want you to parent by choice and not by chance. This will happen as you approach parenting with a little more emotional intelligence, which includes taking a little time to reflect on where you are in your parenting and your life in general, and to become more self-aware of how these various aspects of life influence your relationship with your teenagers.

One thing to remember: There is plenty of time to change. There is no biological window of change that is going to close. Whatever you feel you want to do differently, whatever patterns you want to modify, you can do it. What happened between you and your parents is not a script written in stone for your parenting. But it is harder to change when we are not aware of these patterns and their influence. So read on and fill in more of the picture of where you are in your life and parenting.

YOUR CURRENT LIFE CIRCUMSTANCES

This part of the survey explores your work situation; by "work" here we mean your job or career, volunteer work, or full-time parenting. Place an X over the number that corresponds to how things are now. Circle the number for how things were five years ago.

a. Flexibility:

Very						Not at all
1	2	3	4	5	6	7

b. Satisfaction:

Complete						None
1	2	3	4	5	6	7

c. Stress:

Minimal						Extreme
1	2	3	4	5	6	7

d. Time demands:

Easy						Constant
1	2	3	4	5	6	7

e. Compensation:

Fair						Inadequate
1	2	3	4	5	6	7

f. Enjoyment:

Fun						None
1	2	3	4	5	6	7

g. Coworkers:

Supportive						Undermining
1	2	3	4	5	6	7

h. Hecticness:

Okay						Exhausted
1	2	3	4	5	6	7

What do you like best about your work situation?

What do you like least?

What can you change?

We spend more time working than performing any other single activity. That distinction used to belong to sleep, but that was before the ten-hour workday and the six-hour sleep night. Most of us bring stress from work into our homes as if it were a take-out dinner that lasts and lasts, and this impacts on us and on our family. One of us had a friend who was in a very depressing job; in order to feel better, he began taking antidepressant medication. This seems rather odd, that he would take medication to cope with a stressful situation rather than change the situation, but this is all too common. There are times when we may have to do this, but too often we accept the stress of our jobs without thinking of ways we can make some positive changes (not necessarily getting a new job).

Taking medications might make us better on the job, but it is not likely to be a genuine solution to stress-related problems. Negative feelings have a way of coming in the door with us at the end of the day...something that those of us who remember our little discussion of the brain earlier can understand well. We need to stop and look at how we feel, where we are, and how the two relate. For most of us, it is true that we still have to work, but we can make choices.

For example, think of how things were five or ten years ago. Are you now where you thought you would be today? Is this what you wanted it to be? One interesting thing about being at the point of having teenagers, especially if they are in high school, is that we created a lot of our early career goals before we had kids. Now we can see that there are important family and parenting goals that also require our time. So maybe you won't be the CEO for a while, or start your own small business, or cure cancer. There is a lot you can do and are accomplishing while still being involved in raising your children. We have seen too many parents who can't find the time for their teenagers until they are forced to attend school meetings, drug rehab sessions, or family therapy. Reflect on who you are and where you are in life. Be sure your kids are part of the equation. Of course, as you reflect you might conclude that some sacrifices have to be made, mostly financial ones. But what is sanity worth? What is your relationship with your kids and spouse worth? You decide.

YOUR TEEN'S TEMPERAMENT

Speaking of our teens, let's take a look at the mix of "personalities" in your family. Place an X over the number that corresponds to your teen's characteristic and circle the number that corresponds to your characteristic. Use a different color to circle the number for your spouse. If there are others in your household, rate them also, and if your teens have a stepfamily, you can rate its members, too.

a. Discipline:

Easy						Impossible
1	2	3	4	5	6	7

b. Adaptability:

Flexible						Rigid
1	2	3	4	5	6	7

c. Reactivity:

Easygoing					Quick and Intense	
1	2	3	4	5	6	7

d. Mood:

Good						Bad
1	2	3	4	5	6	7

e. Mood stability:

Stable					Variable	
1	2	3	4	5	6	7

f. Behavior:

Thoughtful					Impulsive	
1	2	3	4	5	6	7

We have asked you to rate different aspects of your temperament. We like to think of temperament as the "factory settings" all of us are born with. Like factory settings, aspects of our temperament can be changed, but it is easier to make these changes earlier in life, and the instruction manual is not always clear on exactly how to proceed. Many of us leave things as they are and then just deal with the aspects we don't like, or simply get used to them.

With a family, though, we have lots of factory settings, and they might not all be compatible. The result? Static. Tones that do not match. Discordance. The teenage years, especially the early teenage years, are a good time to examine those factory settings and perhaps consider making a couple of key adjustments.

Check Your Numbers. Overall on this scale, where is your teen, your spouse, you? Low numbers indicate an "easy" temperament. Kids like this can sometimes raise themselves. No matter what you do in terms of parenting, it seems to work. One of us had a neighbor who came over one day very distraught. When asked what was the matter, she tearfully said that her eight-year-old daughter had said no to her and she did not know what to do. We suggested a donation to a charity as a thank-you for being so blessed. A child who said no for the first time at age eight is likely to be cooperative and thoughtful in most things she does. We are sure that this parent is not reading this book right now, because this child does not present many challenges to the parent. We should add that children like this are very rare. The rest of us have more "normal" kids, who are not so easy.

For those of you who have teens with high numbers on this scale, you have our sympathy. Some kids are just harder than others to raise. We know we did not have to tell you this and that you have known it for some time now, but we want to reassure you that this is not all "your" doing. When kids have a difficult temperament no matter what you do, it is just harder; kids like this tend to learn the hard way. It's not that our words don't matter, but these kids tend to need to experience things for themselves. And some teens need to experience things over and over again that we might think would "teach them a lesson" the first time. Perhaps when they were little, you might tell them to not touch the stove because they would get burnt or not to go in the street without holding an adult's hand, but some kids have to touch or run into the street anyway. This leads to anxiety and sometimes heartache for parents. But we want to reassure you: There is a better-than-average chance that when your tough teenager becomes a parent, his or her kids will do the same kinds of things to them. Revenge!

Look at the Match of Scores. For those of you who find this interesting, we can add a few more things to think about. First of all, consider the match between your scores and those of your teens. If both you and your teen are extroverted, for example, you are likely to see things the same way and share emotional reactions to social situations. This leads to mutual understanding and lower degrees of conflict.

But nothing is simple, is it? Sometimes when we are on the same emotional wavelength as our teens, we overidentify with them. We see too much of ourselves in them. We sometimes ask them to carry hopes and dreams from our own lives that we did not have a chance to reach. Perhaps we want them to be a more perfect version of ourselves. They are going to be us but smarter, more accomplished, happier. Or we see in our teen things we do not like in ourselves. We can have too much concern about changing traits in our teens (anxiety, moodiness, low anger threshold, a tendency to be overweight, and so on) that remind us of what we think of as our own shortcomings.

These are not "abnormal" reactions of parents to teenagers. But as we discussed earlier, adolescents need to establish their *own* identity. Sometimes they take on identities too soon or for the wrong reasons, such as trying to meet their parents' needs. No matter how similar our teen is to us, we have to keep in mind that they are their own person, for good and for bad. Strengths they have are their strengths, and weaknesses they have are their weaknesses. We want to work with our teens and their characteristics, but they are not direct extensions of us. They need room to grow.

Teens Don't Have to Be What You Want. If, however, there are mismatches in your ratings, these can lead to misunderstanding and a lack of empathy with the other party. It is natural to think that what feels "right" to us is in fact right. But this is not always the case. Sometimes, it's like flavors of ice cream. We like what we like and can't imagine others liking certain things. Butter pecan? Yucch! But your teen might like it. It's not for us to understand all these preferences.

Most examples are harder. Some teenagers appear to be disorganized and chaotic. Some parents might find this unacceptable. They cannot imagine living that way or how anyone *could* live that way. They see such teens as wasting lots of time, time that could be used to organize, put things away, prepare for the next day, dust, whatever. A parent might feel that this is not an issue of temperament or comfort, but something essential for success in life. How can work get done and career and family responsibilities get managed in a state of disorganization?

It's a hard reality to accept that some quite wonderful and successful people and terrific parents are disorganized slobs. It's also true that some people never reach their potential because of personal chaos. But it's hard to know in advance what is going to happen. Is it worth all the nagging that it takes to change a temperament and characteristic that is not to your liking? Is it worth jeopardizing your relationship with your teenager? Again, each parent must arrive at his or her own answers. We will say, however, that our clinical business is overpopulated by parents who no longer have relationships with their teens because they could not get their teens to change and be the people the parents felt they needed to be to have a happy future. One of our colleagues, a deep theoretician, has applied his many years of education and practice to this issue. His conclusion: When life gives you lemons, sometimes the best thing to do is make lemonade.

As you are reaching for your favorite headache remedy, we want to make sure you use maximum strength: So now compare you teen with your spouse's (or your former spouse's) temperament. How are they similar or dissimilar? What do you like about them both? Dislike about them both? Your current relationship with your teenager's other parent can complicate this. If there are problems in your relationship with your spouse (or ex) and you see your spouse in your child, obviously, this can be a source of the most difficult problems to get past. Often, personal reflection in these circumstances needs to be supplemented by professional help. Don't delay. Some things are just too tough to work through on our own.

YOUR SUPPORT SYSTEM

Now that you have done some self-reflection and a bit of reflecting on relationships within your family, we want you to take a look at your support system. Your ability to make the changes you want depends on your own personal motivation *and* the demands and resources from your support system. The areas we find most useful to look at are our nonteen children, our relationship with our spouse, our career circumstances, and our general support system. We will conclude with a look at your E.Q. resources.

OUR OTHER CHILDREN

Use a different color to indicate your ratings for each of your nonteen children. You might want to use invisible ink if you think too many 7's are going on the chart.

a. Disciplining:

Easy						Impossible
1	2	3	4	5	6	7

b. Problems:

None						Overwhelming
1	2	3	4	5	6	7

c. Demands on us:

Independent						Demanding
1	2	3	4	5	6	7

d. Enjoyment:

	Fun to be with					Obnoxious
I	2	3	4	5	6	7

e. Closeness:

	Comfortable					None/too close
I	2	3	4	5	6	7

f. Relationship:

	Positive					Negative
I	2	3	4	5	6	7

g. Relationship to siblings:

	Positive					Negative
I	2	3	4	5	6	7

Are our other children a source of pleasure or difficulty, and to what degree?

What are the dynamics like among all family members?

THE OTHER PARENT
(WHETHER WE ARE MARRIED OR NOT)

There is no ink safe enough to use if you find too many 7's on this scale. You might not even want to read this section in public. We recommend a flashlight and a closet.

a. Supportive:

	Very					Undermining
I	2	3	4	5	6	7

b. Closeness to us:

	Intimate					Isolated
I	2	3	4	5	6	7

c. Emotional support:

	Supportive					Uninvolved
I	2	3	4	5	6	7

d. Time together:

	Frequent					None
I	2	3	4	5	6	7

e. Communication:

Good						None
I	2	3	4	5	6	7

f. Sharing of chores:

Equal						None
I	2	3	4	5	6	7

g. Ability to coparent:

On same page						Different books
I	2	3	4	5	6	7

As we implied earlier when looking at the match of temperaments, a positive relationship and the ability to work together with the other parent are crucial for parenting any child. Not only does consistency between the parents help a child learn but lack of consistency undermines a child's feeling of security. This can only worsen as the child enters adolescence. If the teen is able to divide and conquer or, worse, cause conflict between the parents, we are going to have a real problem.

YOUR SOCIAL WORLD

Your social world can be an incredible source of strength to you. It is also a source of many of the linkages that can be so helpful to our teens. Take a good look. You might find that some supports you were not interested in or willing to cultivate for your own personal reasons might now look more appealing as ways to help your teens have more connections with the world and with helpful people. Time spent in developing a better support system often pays unexpected dividends in our ability to be emotionally intelligent parents of our teenagers. We focus here on friends, community, and school.

a. Our friends:

Close						None
I	2	3	4	5	6	7

b. Community:

	Sense of belonging					Isolated
1	2	3	4	5	6	7

c. Shared values:

	Consistent					Contrary
1	2	3	4	5	6	7

d. School environment:

	Healthy					Dangerous
1	2	3	4	5	6	7

e. School resources:

	Available					None
1	2	3	4	5	6	7

f. School pressure:

	Appropriate					Too little/too much
1	2	3	4	5	6	7

g. Approach to discipline:

	Fair					Harsh/overly lenient
1	2	3	4	5	6	7

YOUR EMOTIONAL INTELLIGENCE

YOUR EMOTIONAL RANGE: FIGHT-OR-FLIGHT OR WHAT?

How often do you display the following feelings toward your children:

	Always	Regularly	Once in a While	Rarely	Never
Love	1	2	3	4	5
Pride	1	2	3	4	5
Fun	1	2	3	4	5
Compassion	1	2	3	4	5
Respect	1	2	3	4	5
Understanding	1	2	3	4	5
Interest	1	2	3	4	5

Anger	1	2	3	4	5
Disappointment	1	2	3	4	5
Frustration	1	2	3	4	5
Annoyance	1	2	3	4	5
Embarrassment	1	2	3	4	5
Anxiety	1	2	3	4	5
Withdrawal	1	2	3	4	5

We list positive feelings first because many people forget about these. What is the balance between positive and negative feelings? Do we enjoy our teen? It's hard to live with someone we do not like, and even harder to parent them. It's also important to show our teenagers a decent emotional range. They need to know that there is a balance of Love, Laughter, and Limits. How do these feelings impact on our relationship with our teen and with other family members? Do positive or negative feelings overflow onto others? What feelings would we like to change?

How does our teen push our buttons? Note those that seem familiar:

Argue
Not talk
Hang out with friends we disapprove of
Refuse to engage in family activities
Act disrespectfully
Deliberately violate house rules
Fail in school or underachieve
Show lack of consideration for family but not friends
Dress inappropriately
Insist on body alteration such as tattoos, piercing, and/or stupid
    haircuts
Listen to annoying music, usually too loud

Believe it or not, all these actions are relatively normal. (Hey, we did this stuff too...except if our parents or kids are reading this, in which case we are just kidding.) Of course, it is a matter of degree. We did not put drug use, violence, or sexual promiscuity on this list because while these can be a part of adolescence, they are not okay. You need to decide what you can tolerate and what you cannot. Your teens are going to do at least some of the things listed above, so accept it. Do not just react with horror. Think about where and how you are going to set limits, but realize you cannot control everything. As the Serenity Prayer says: "God grant me the serenity to accept the things I cannot change, the strength to change the things I can, and the wisdom to know the difference." In this book, we will help you with the wisdom part and, hopefully, by looking at your life circumstances you can work on the serenity part. And now for strengths.

YOUR E.Q. PARENTING STRENGTHS

To what extent would you say you:

a. Are aware of kids', spouse's feelings:

This is definitely me		Sort of me	Definitely not me	
I	2	3	4	5

b. Show a high degree of self-control with teens:

This is definitely me		Sort of me	Definitely not me	
I	2	3	4	5

c. Possess a strong sense of empathy with teens:

This is definitely me		Sort of me	Definitely Not me	
I	2	3	4	5

d. Are great at seeing other family members' points of view:

This is definitely me		Sort of me	Definitely not me	
I	2	3	4	5

e. Set positive goals for teens, family:

This is definitely me		Sort of me	Definitely not me	
I	2	3	4	5

f. Do organized, detailed planning around parenting tasks:

This is definitely me		Sort of me	Definitely not me	
I	2	3	4	5

   g. Act in highly effective, comfortable ways with my teenagers:

This is definitely me		Sort of me	Definitely not me	
1	2	3	4	5

   h. Resolve household conflicts peacefully:

This is definitely me		Sort of me	Definitely not me	
1	2	3	4	5

   i. Use creative problem solving around parenting issues:

This is definitely me		Sort of me	Definitely not me	
1	2	3	4	5

On the road to bringing Love, Laughter, Limits, and Linkages into our teens' lives, our Emotionally Intelligent Parenting strengths are the frame of our vehicle. A vehicle is no stronger than its frame, and we never lose sight of the fact that one cannot infer much about a frame by looking only at the outer body of the vehicle. Therefore, you need to honestly appraise your own strengths when it comes to using your E.Q. skills in parenting. That's why we are focusing beyond our earlier "refresher" look at your overall E.Q. skills. When it comes to parenting, what is "definitely you"? What is "sort of you"? What is "not you"? Would your kids agree? Would your teen's other parent agree? If you are courageous, ask them! The feedback can only help!

Regardless, keep this inventory of your strengths. By the time you read and put into practice ideas from this book, we expect you are going to get better at your strengths and improve in those areas in which you wish to improve.

Look back also at what pushes your buttons. The big question for you is to what extent you use your strengths during those moments of stress. The first thing we can ask of ourselves is to put our best skills to use at the toughest times. We all make mistakes; it's impossible to avoid them. But we can offset a lot with how we put our assets to use. In Part 2, we will give you some tools to use to bring your Emotionally Intelligent Parenting to the next level.

Part 2

■   ■   ■

A TOOLBOX FOR THE EMOTIONALLY INTELLIGENT PARENTING OF YOUR TEENS

If your only tool is a hammer, you treat everything like a nail.

—SOME WISE CARPENTER

FOR MANY PARENTS, DIFFICULTY IN WORKING WITH TEENS ARISES because they do not have the right tools for the job. You may still be using tools from childhood, which no longer work. Teens are more complex and often require a different approach. You used to be able to get away with using "time out" for nearly everything; perhaps just the threat of loss of video-game privileges could nail the child to the floor; or maybe he or she responded to "the look." If you tried these now, you would be met with a big "So what?" Your hammer is not broken and your screwdriver is not bent; these just are not the tools for this particular job.

In previous chapters, we have discussed what you need to give your teens (Love, Laughter, Limits, and Linkages), how this will help teens meet their developmental needs for Appreciation, Belonging, Competencies and Confidence, and Contributions (A, B, and the three C's), and how all this relates to the principles of Emotionally Intelligent Parenting. In this chapter, we will give you some tools for tuning up parent-teen interactions in a way that preserves a positive, constructive relationship. We will also talk about "discipline" in this section, but in doing so we will emphasize teaching teenagers the skills of emotional intelligence. This is the best way we know to foster self-discipline.

DO YOU HAVE ESP?

You've likely realized by now that we are into acronyms. These give us a quick way to remember what to do in stressful situations. Also, we know that the simpler the concept, the more likely it is to be implemented, especially in emotionally charged situations. So here is another acronym to keep in mind when you confront a troubling parenting situation with your teen: ESP.

You fans of the *X-Files* and similar programs might quickly assume we are referring to extrasensory perception. It certainly is true that this kind of ESP is helpful for Enlightened Sensitive Parenting to create Extraordinarily Successful People, but this is really an Entirely Superficial Point.

To us, ESP means: **Evaluate, Select,** and **Proceed.**

When interacting with our teens, it may seem like we need extrasensory perception in order to know what they are thinking and what to do. Don't worry; you do not have to read their minds, consult crystal balls, or call the psychic hotline. However, you do need to use our version of ESP. ESP will come in handy when you are interacting with teens in stressful situations, helping them make decisions, or, often, just trying to talk to them.

Chapter 6

ESP, FLASH, and Other Emotionally Intelligent Parenting Tools in Your Toolbox

EVALUATE

First, you want to **evaluate** the situation. We need to size up not only what is happening but the feelings and perspectives of those involved. We also want to manage our own feelings and be sure we are not reacting impulsively or to some aspect of the situation that is more relevant to our own past than to our teens' present and future.

YOUR FEELINGS, FEELINGS FINGERPRINTS, TRIGGER SITUATIONS: WHAT IS GOING ON HERE?

Start with your feelings. How are you feeling about this situation or problem? What chords is it striking in you? Try to differentiate your own feelings—are you angry or are you worried? When your teen comes home at 3:00 A.M., it may be a little difficult to be in touch with your feelings of concern, but this is most likely what underlies your expression of anger.

Be aware of how your body tells you what you are feeling. Do you get headaches, are your muscles tight, is your stomach upset? Tuning in to your body's stress indicators can make it easier for you to identify them and catch them early, before they are out of control. We call these "feelings fingerprints" "or "stress signatures," because we all have different ways our bodies tell us we are under stress, and we need to recognize our particular signs.

You also want to recognize the situations that can lead to a strong emotional reaction, such as seeing a new body piercing or having your daughter's new boyfriend appear in person or, even worse, encountering both at the same time. These are "trigger situations." When we identify these ahead of time, we can be more prepared to deal with them in a thoughtful manner once the situation is upon us. For example, Saturday morning may be a "trigger situation." It is 11:00 A.M., Sheila is still asleep, you have things to do, you know Sheila must have things to do, and you know that when she wakes up, she is going to ask you to do something for her, like make breakfast or say, "Quick, you have to take me to the mall to meet Stacy!" People are usually at their worst when they are blindsided, because this is when emotional hijackings occur. You can identify a trigger situation mostly by history; in other words, if it happened before, it is likely to happen again. After about a month of Saturday morning arguments, you should begin to catch on to the pattern.

The following is a list of common trigger situations for parents. Please feel free to E-mail us at www.EQParenting.com with a list of your own.

- The morning routine or the lack of one: getting up in the morning, getting to school on time, organizing oneself, eating breakfast, family interactions when everyone's rushing
- Dealing with extracurricular activities: the schlepping, driving, waiting, and so on. What is too much? How should you prioritize teens' activities and your job?
- Chores: The room—to clean or not to clean? Laundry: who will do it? Is anyone helping out in the household?
- Homework: how much to be involved, how to monitor, issues of quality and quantity
- The nightly routine: bedtime, phone use, Internet use
- Weekends: curfew, social activities, family time, drugs
- Dating: when and how much, who, sex

- Money: allowance, accountability
- Friends: peer pressure, how much control to try to have
- School: grades, course selection, discipline
- Thinking about the future: What do they want to be when they grow up? What does the family want them to be when they grow up?

YOUR TEENAGERS' FEELINGS

Another important tool in this category is to be aware of our teens' feelings. This is hard to do, especially when we are upset. Our reactions to our teens can be so intense that we can lose track of what might be going on with them. That's why it's crucial, even if only for a little while, to step back after a difficult encounter and try to understand what our teens are feeling. What is their perspective on what has happened? What were they feeling? Might you have read the situation incorrectly?

Sometimes we get into a "two wrongs make a right" rut. We'll wonder how our children can be so insensitive to us, and we might find ourselves saying, "Why should I be considerate to him? He doesn't think about my feelings at all." Unfortunately, as the parent, you don't have the luxury of dwelling on these kinds of thoughts for too long. It is your job to take care of your children, and the way to do this is by understanding them. Yes, we want them to be aware of and sensitive to your feelings, but this will come only after you have modeled this for them and empathized with them.

It is important to attend to nonverbal cues in divining your teens' feelings. What is their body language telling you? What is their facial expression? Listen to their tone of voice as well as the content of what they are saying. Keep in mind that often the best defense is a good offense, and your teens may be on the offensive because they are really feeling guilt or sadness. Getting past your own upset feelings often leads to productive connections with your teens.

IT'S 10:00 P.M.—DO YOU KNOW WHICH CHANNEL YOUR TEENAGER IS BROADCASTING ON?

In this age of the media, we like to use television and computer analogies to help you be more on target in understanding your teens. They are at different places at different times. Part of our problem as parents is tuning in to where they are and responding appropriately.

Teenagers often send out signals that let their parents know how they are feeling and what they most need. These signals differ, depending on the issue or problem and on what the teenagers are looking for from their parents (or other adults they respect and with whom they have open channels of communication). As parents learn which channel their teenager is broadcasting on, the reception becomes clearer. There is less static, and the message can be received and responded to accurately. Here is a quick listing of your teenager's broadcast channels, followed by a more in-depth guide. Notice that they give us an acronym, FLASH (sorry, we could not help throwing in another one):

Channel F: I need to save *face.*
Channel L: Please *listen* to me.
Channel A: I am looking for an *argument.*
Channel S: I need *support.*
Channel H: I need *help.*

Channel F: I Need to Save Face. For reasons we have discussed earlier, teenagers are prone to suffer embarrassment. Sometimes peers are the cause, but family members can also bring forth feelings of shame or resentment. (He's such a good piano player. Play for Uncle Leo and Aunt Bea. Come on. He'll play, he loves to. Won't you play? Be nice and play. *Play now!*). Channel F is relevant when teenagers have to deal with some revelation or incident that exposed an imperfection or two. Channel F might also be on if your teenager avoids seeing certain people or rejects certain phone calls. You show your love and support by helping them save face, not by pushing them into further embarrassment. Channel H is more general; it covers lots of situations but most often focuses on your child and some task or object. Channel F is a public channel; it involves other people and is focused on a very limited program content: how to save face. Let us note here that we are talking about your teens' feeling embarrassed about themselves. It is taken for granted that they feel embarrassed about you. There is no known cure for this.

Channel L: Please Listen to Me. You can tell that Channel L is on when your teenager approaches you about talking, or leaves an opening that suggests something is the matter. (Oh, nothing ... really, things went fine. Well, I guess they went okay. How am I? I'm, uhh, great, sort of.) It is important to listen to silence as well; if your teen is hanging out around you and *not* talking, this can also be a sign that she really does want to communicate something. This is why parenting can be time-consuming and not time-efficient. Sometimes you need to allow for hanging-around time. It would be great if everyone would communicate what they needed to have in a nice, neat, brief time slot, but they do not, and teens in particular do not.

Most often, your child will have some confusion or indecision that he or she thinks could benefit from being talked about. Remember, Channel L is not "Please tell me what to do." It's "Please *listen* to me." By listening and eliciting information about their feelings and perspective, you will keep the channel open and perhaps help your teenagers resolve whatever concerns them.

Channel A: I'm Looking for an Argument. It will not surprise you to know that this channel is accompanied by static. Signs of Channel A include surly or oppositional behavior, challenges to your authority, negative statements, and, our favorite, lots of negative body language. Nothing you say is right or even acceptable. Why is this happening? Do not look for deep reasons. Sometimes teens are filled with upset or even just boisterous or contentious feelings; they simply may be looking for an argument. Parents whose teenagers are broadcasting on Channel A but *think* their children are broadcasting on Channel S (I need support) or L (please listen) are in for a particularly tough time. The longer you tune in to A, the more likely it is you will be drawn into a conflict. Sometimes *you* may be looking for a good argument, but if you are not, then you will want to open up other channels.

Warning: You cannot switch your teens from Channel A to any other channel; only *they* can switch. They control the remote. You cannot even press the mute button. Your only choices are to wait for a commercial break, suffer through to the end of the show, get up and leave the room, or let them know you do not want to watch this show but would like to watch another channel with them, preferably S (support) or H (help).

Channel S: I Need Support. For even the most well-adjusted teenager, there will be times when the going gets rough. Perhaps Charlie had a difficult exam or a bad game or got into an argument with a friend. If there is a new challenge being faced, you may detect some uncertainty in your adolescent. When Robin shows signs of being concerned, down, or a bit uptight, you are probably receiving broadcasts from her on Channel S. The most effective method of expressing support is to use the questioning techniques and paraphrasing discussed on pages 121–123.

Channel H: I Need Help. Oh, if only our teens would turn to this channel more often! There is nothing more gratifying for a parent to hear than "Mom, Dad, I need your help." This is why we had children in the first place, to provide guidance, to help them grow, to create perfect versions of ourselves.

Disappointingly to parents, Channel H is usually activated only during some very specific task, such as fixing a bicycle or a car or doing a homework assignment, and not for the biggies, like What should I be when I grow up? When do you think I'll be ready to become involved in a serious relationship? How can I organize my life to perform to the best of my abilities and meet all of the expectations you have for me?

Your teen is probably tuning to Channel H when you notice clear signs of frustration, like the slamming down of a pen or tools, perhaps some groaning, or even "I give up." While your crystal ball may tell you to say, "I'll help you" or "I didn't think you could do it," we believe that ESP is better than a crystal ball. So try to hold off your immediate reactions and read below about how to select and carry out good approaches to such situations.

EMPATHY AND PARAPHRASING

Once you have tuned in to your teens' feelings and needs, or at least made a valiant attempt, empathize. Express and show your understanding of how they are feeling and what they are saying. One way of doing this is through paraphrasing. Simply express back to them, without evaluation or ESP or FLASH techniques, how they say they are feeling and what they think. ("You said you are really frustrated and don't think your teachers care about you.") Again, empathizing does not mean you agree. Often just this simple act of understanding goes a long way to opening the door of communication and solving the problem. One of the most important things to all of us is the simple act of being listened to, really heard, and understood. It feels deeply good when this happens. It somehow relieves us of the emotional burden we were feeling even though nothing actually happened. Parenting is hard enough. This is one of those simple, easy-to-use tools; when used every day, it is probably the most powerful one in your toolbox. (By the way, this works equally well with your spouse, boss, employees, and anyone else you want to get along with.)

QUESTIONING TECHNIQUES

Another key skill in evaluating the situation is to ask questions. The more you ask, the more you will know and the more the situation will be clarified for your teen as well. You will want to avoid the question, "Why?"—which is not a request for information, but is often perceived as an accusation and therefore causes defensiveness. "Why did you do that?" will automatically cause your teen to either withdraw or get angry. Also, we like to point out, the common answer to the "why" question is "I don't know," "Because I felt like it," or silence. But the correct answer is usually a variation of "Well, you know, Dad, sometimes I neglect to thoroughly analyze the situation, evaluate possible alternatives, and anticipate the consequences of my actions." We have heard the "why" question many times but have rarely actually heard a teenager—or anyone else, for that matter—give the right answer.

Instead of "why," ask "what" questions. What are you feeling? What do you think I am feeling? What do you want to have happen? What is your goal in this situation? What have you tried and what other things can you think of doing? What do you think might happen if you continue to proceed with what you're doing?

It is important to ask *open-ended questions* rather than closed questions. "Please tell me what happened" works better than "Why do you always pick on your brother?" We do not want to assume things. Instead of initially trying to guess what the problem is or what your teen is feeling, give him a chance to say it in his own way. We are trying to get our teens to think for themselves, and the more you ask, the more they will think.

In addition to an open-ended question, you generally want to *follow up a question with another question;* we call this the two-question rule. It reminds you to stay in a questioning mode. Ask, for example, "How did you feel after she said that?" After your teen answers, try "How else did you feel?" or "How do you think she felt?"

We also recommend that you use the Columbo technique. This is named for the Peter Falk character on television, Lieutenant Columbo (we hope he stays on the air, because we watch him for research and training purposes). Lieutenant Columbo, in a confused and disarming way, asks obvious or simplistic questions to help him understand exactly what is going on. By doing this, he either gets the one little clue that helps him solve the case or he traps the suspect in an inconsistency that leads to self-incrimination. For example, you could ask your teen directly,

"Why are you home so late?" and invite a long and winding excuse and/or argument. Or you could ask, "What time is it? I thought you said you would be home by ten. What happened? Where did you say you were going?"

Overall, there is an inverse relationship between the amount of talking a parent does and the amount of *listening* a teenager does. Remember back to when you were an adolescent and your parent was giving you a lecture. It might have been Lecture No. 23: "If You Do Not Keep Your Room Clean Then How Do You Expect to Live with Anyone, Do You Think Your Wife Will Clean Up After You, Well You Have a Big Surprise in Store for You, Young Man" (this is the short title). As a teenager, did you listen when you were being lectured to? We doubt it. Today's teens have even less tolerance for "the Lecture." By questioning rather than lecturing, you increase the likelihood of being listened to.

These questioning, understanding, and empathizing tools give you a way of evaluating the situation for yourself and your teen. It is important that you keep your cool through the whole process of doing this. We are sure that we do not have to tell you that your emotional reaction can be like gasoline on a fire. Your mantra should be "Keep calm, keep calm, keep calm!"

KEEP CALM

One technique for keeping calm is an activity called, not surprisingly, Keep Calm. This is a breathing technique adapted from Lamaze. We figure that if it helps women get through childbirth, it can help people get through their children's adolescence, although certainly the stress of adolescence lasts a lot longer. You will want to use Keep Calm when you feel your feelings fingerprints or when you are in a trigger situation.

Here are the Keep Calm steps:

1. Say to yourself, "Stop, keep calm."
2. Breathe in through your nose to a count of five.
3. Hold that breath for a count of two.

4. Breathe out through your mouth to a count of five.
5. Repeat as necessary.

It is also okay to walk away and come back when you are calm.

THE 24-KARAT GOLDEN RULE

Although we mentioned this in Chapter 1, it's good to take a more detailed look at how it operates as a tool in your tool kit. One thing that might help you keep calm when raising an adolescent (no, we don't mean Demerol) is to remember that you love this person. You do not want to hurt him or her in any way. Think about how you want others to treat your child. Our 24-Karat Golden Rule for parenting in this century is "Do unto your children as you would have other people do unto your children." Often we find ourselves treating our own children in ways that if others did the same, we would be calling the state child-protection agency or a lawyer. Unintentionally, parents find themselves saying hurtful things to their children and putting them down. This is usually when we are parenting with the emotional part of our brain rather than the thinking part. If we can keep in mind how we expect others to treat our teen, then this can sometimes give us the objectivity we need to treat our teen in a more appropriate and effective manner. Remember the Neighbor Test!

Ask yourself and your teen: How can we do this in a calm way without it leading to a blowup? How are we going to talk to each other? Are sarcasm, anger, and put-downs okay? Rolling of the eyes? Pointing and shaking of the finger? Is this a good time and place or do we need a better one? How do you want me to treat you? How do you think I want to be treated so this works out best?

SELECT

After **evaluating** the situation in a calm way, we want to **select** our course of action and help our teens select theirs. Throughout this book you will note a duality of purpose: by using these skills you are modeling and teaching your teen to use these skills as well. Most of your teaching will be done by example. Unfortunately, gone are the days when you could sit your child down and say, "Now we are going to learn how to solve problems." Sorry, you missed your chance. You should have bought our previous book when your child was younger. It might not be too late: *Emotionally Intelligent Parenting: How to Raise a Self-Disciplined, Responsible, Socially Skilled Child* is now available in paperback.

BE POSITIVE

Selecting a course of action involves setting goals and planning. First and foremost, though, we want to be positive and focus on strengths. What are our strengths, the strengths of our family, and our teen's strengths? What resources can we draw on? In what ways is the cup half full? There is something depressing about parenting models that focus on deficit reduction (maybe it's the political and economic association that this has). Who wants to deal with deficiencies and problems? Certainly not your teen. It is always important to view a situation from a positive perspective. What is it that you are working toward? What do you want to have happen? Goals are stated positively. This gives a sense of hope and optimism, a vision of what we want to achieve. We are certainly not being Pollyannaish about this. We recognize the seriousness of many teenage problems and know that some of them are real risk factors. Focusing on the negative, however, will rarely motivate positive change. It usually only discourages everyone.

PROBLEM SOLVING AND DECISION MAKING

The model that we use for selecting a course of action is represented by the acronym FIG TESPN (pronounced FIG TESS-pin). This is not a cookie named for a Norwegian explorer but a process that you can use to guide yourself and your teens when dealing with difficult situations, problems, and decisions. Do not worry about memorizing this process, along with all the other information we have given you. There will not be a quiz, although your kids tend to test you every day. We want you to be aware of the whole process in detail, but primarily we expect you to use the methods that you personally find most helpful.

FIG TESPN stands for:

F: Feelings cue me to problem solving.
I: I have a problem.
G: Goals give me a guide.

T: Think of things to do.
E: Envision outcomes.
S: Select a solution.
P: Plan and be prepared for pitfalls.
N: Now what?

We have already covered the importance of being aware of your feelings. But not only do you want to notice your feelings and control them, you also want to view them as a cue to engage in problem solving. Bad feelings let you know that there is a problem and you need to so something about it. It is like physical pain. If you exert yourself and feel pain in some part of your body that will not go away, it is not just a sign of age but also a sign that something may be wrong. If you do not do something about it, it is likely that the pain will not go away and may get worse.

Emotional pain works the same way. If you find yourself angry, frustrated, or worried, this means that there is a problem and you need to do something. And this something is not to act on the negative emotion or deny it but to engage in problem solving.

"I have a problem" means that it is important to decide whose problem it is. If it is your problem, then you need to do something about it. As a parent, it may seem to be your problem for one of two reasons. Either it really is your problem and not your teen's, or it is your teen's problem but becomes your problem because you are her parent. Sometimes, it may be your problem and not your teen's because you are overidentifying with her. In other words, if she fails a test, it becomes your problem because you feel like you have failed, not her. The focus of this problem is your feeling of failure and your expectation of yourself as a parent, rather than the child's academic performance.

It can also be your problem because you are responsible for your teen. If your teen is drinking, this is certainly a problem for him, but also a problem for you because you need to do something about it. You cannot sit back and allow your son to work it out himself. The stakes are too great.

Differentiating whose problem it is can be difficult. The way to look at it is to ask, Who is responsible for fixing it? In the first example, the teen is responsible for grades, not the parent. In the second example, the parent needs to take responsibility not for causing the problem of drinking but for doing something about it. Speaking of drinking, it may help if you keep the Serenity Prayer from Alcoholics Anonymous in mind; it applies to raising emotionally intelligent teenagers, as well as to the rest of life: "God grant me the strength to change the things I can, the serenity to accept the things I cannot, and the wisdom to know the difference."

So, what is our goal? What do we want to have happen? What is our teen's goal? How can we both get what we want? Where do we start? We need to be realistic about our goals and help our teens be realistic about theirs. Think about what it is you really want for them. Remember to focus on long-term goals, not just short-term. For example, sometimes through threat of punishment you can get teens to study or clean their room, but is this really your goal? Maybe your goal is to get them to be independent and responsible; if this is your goal, then threatening may not be the best way to achieve your end.

Your adolescents also need to be aware of their goals. Sometimes, when asked for a goal, teens may say, "I don't know," "I don't have any," or "Don't sweat it," but, of course, you are not reassured by any of this. Try to get them to see that by setting a goal they have a better chance of achieving something, ideally something they care about. As we noted earlier, their goals are a way of obtaining Appreciation, Belonging, and Competence and Confidence, and of making Contributions. Some teens are resistant to setting goals because they anticipate failure no matter what they do. Sometimes you have to address this directly and then set a small goal, to get them started.

For example, a high school senior may procrastinate about college admissions because of fear of rejection. In this case, you should fill out the application and write the essays for them...just kidding. What you should do is hire someone to do it for them... still kidding. (What is not funny is that some parents actually do this.) Actually, we suggest that you ask what you can do to offer support or that you encourage them to think about which part of the large task they might be able to do over the coming weekend. They do not have to do the whole application, but they can identify a part they think they can realistically complete by Sunday. Helping them set a small but obtainable goal is much preferable to nagging or threatening. Once they have accomplished something tangible, they begin to experience success and see that the task is not so daunting.

After setting goals comes "thinking of things to do," or generating options to achieve one's goals. Again, this holds true for parents as well as teens. We encourage you, and we encourage you to encourage your teen, to think creatively of lots of different things to do. Brainstorm. Sometimes ideas that seem way out or unworkable or wild can help you think of good ideas, so try to give all ideas a hearing. Effective solutions are not always obvious. What is more obvious is an ineffective solution. Allow yourself to brainstorm your way out of unsuccessful strategies. In the workplace, we would never even think of repeatedly using ineffective ways to solve a problem, but somehow, in parenting, we tend to do this. This is because we sometimes let our emotional brains overwhelm our thinking brains.

Of course, after thinking of something to do, we need to envision, or imagine, what might happen. If we try to ground our teen, what might happen? Maybe he will only become more resentful and antagonistic, or maybe he will begin to grasp the fact that we are really serious and this is one limit that cannot be challenged. We do not know what the outcomes are; you know your teen better than anyone does. It is necessary to try to envision what might happen if you do something.

A parallel process is to help your teen see what might happen if she does something. Teens tend to be poor at envisioning consequences, especially long-term consequences. They tend to focus on immediate gratification. This can be dangerous, as when they rationalize smoking by telling themselves, "I won't get lung cancer until I'm middle-aged, and I can quit before then." It is often necessary for parents to help teens envision the future, even when they deny its existence.

In selecting a solution, one must be mindful of the goal. It is interesting how often we get distracted from what we are trying to do. We think about things, and this makes us think about other things, and before we know it, we do not know what we started thinking about. You need to stay focused and to help your children stay focused on their goals and then decide what to do based on their goals.

In addition to goals, we need plans to help us reach them. What is your plan? What can you do? What are you willing to do? An important part of any plan is to develop contingency strategies; in other words, what will you do when obstacles to the plan arise or things do not go as anticipated? In the above college application example, your plan is to offer assistance and support and help your teen set realistic goals. An obstacle to the plan might be that your spouse does not agree with your plan and starts to yell at your son to get his "lazy ass" in gear and do the applications or else you will not send him to college at all. Try to anticipate these obstacles and deal with them beforehand, such as by talking with your spouse in order to present a united front.

Now what? Reflect on your actions and encourage your teenagers to reflect on theirs. Did you and they get what they want? How does everyone feel now? Is it necessary to go back and select a different option? Was the goal realistic? If it worked, great, let's remember it for next time. If not, that's okay, try something else.

PROCEED

Finally, after we **evaluate** our feelings and the situation and **select** our goal and plan, we are ready to **proceed**. We have to do *something!* All this understanding and planning are great, but now you have to actually talk to your teenager. When doing so, keep in mind your feelings, use the questioning techniques, and engage in problem solving. But you also want to:

BE YOUR BEST

BEST is another of our cute little acronyms that help remind you of a complex set of skills. We mentioned it earlier as part of the basic principles of Emotionally Intelligent Parenting. It stands for:

  B: Body language: What are your nonverbal body cues telling your teen? Are you hovering over them or standing in a threatening manner? Are you a little too relaxed or standing firm? Your body posture can convey a great deal about how seriously you take something and whether you are open to communication or closed to it.

  E: Eye contact or lack thereof: Many times we are so distracted, we do not even realize that we are not looking at the person we are speaking to. We might be talking to our teen while cooking dinner, reading the mail, or watching TV. Obviously, this is not conducive to communication. In our hectic lives, there are too many times when we are talking to someone but we are not really there, mentally. We are still at work, thinking of all the aggravations that occurred or thinking ahead to all the things still left to do. It is important to stop and look at teenagers when talking with them. You will know that you have not done this for a while if, in response to your making eye contact, your teen immediately says, "What are you staring at?" in a suspicious way.

S: Say appropriate things: This is harder to do than it seems, but it certainly helps if you remember to stay calm. Criticism, sarcasm, condescension, disrespect, nagging, and pleading cannot be considered appropriate things. Say how you feel and what you mean in a direct way. Talk about yourself rather than making accusations of your teen. For example, "It is really important to me that we have a clean house, and I would appreciate your help with this. When you eat something, please put the dishes in the dishwasher so I will not have as much work to do at night." This works much better than, "You are so lazy. You never do anything around here. What do you think, I'm your personal maid? When will you ever learn to be responsible?"

T: Tone of voice: Be conscious of what you say and how you say it. People can use a hurtful tone of voice to upset others without actually saying anything inappropriate. Be mindful of this. Try to be sincere. As George Burns once said, "If you can fake sincerity, you've got it made."

Remember to use these skills when interacting with your teen. And be mindful of what you are modeling.

CONTRACTS

Another tool that is especially powerful when working with teens is contracts. Contracts are negotiated agreements that clearly delineate the responsibilities of all parties and the consequences that will result, both positive and negative. The contract is similar to a behavior chart that you may have used with your younger children, perhaps for toilet training, chores, or how they treated a sibling. The primary difference between a behavior chart and a contract is also the primary difference between childhood and adolescence: The parent has less control and the adolescent has more of a say.

This is good, by the way, because we want children to become more independent and take more responsibility for themselves.

When developing a contract, it is important for all parties to state their goals. The parents' goal may be for the teens to complete their homework and keep their room clean. The teens' goal may be to get the parents off their back and to have fun. The relationship between the parents' and the teens' goals can then be developed. Usually this is put into an "If...then" format: "If you complete your homework in a satisfactory manner during the week, then you can hang out with your friends on Saturday."

It is important to use motivators that your child actually wants, such as time with friends, material goods, or use of the family car. While we always hope that teens' internal values and their relationships with their parents will guide their behavior, we also have to be realists, and sometimes it is necessary to rely on extrinsic motivation. We do not mean bribes but things that they want other than to feel good about themselves and receive love from us. This is part of the way the world works. One reason most of us do our jobs is to get a paycheck.

The monitoring of the contract is important. Without frequent and accurate monitoring, the contract is worthless or, worse, can lead to an increase in conflict if there is disagreement over what various people actually did or did not do. Someone has to take responsibility for monitoring, and it is easier to do so if the goals are clear and measurable. If you are monitoring school performance, you may need to involve the school. If you are monitoring something at home, make sure you are around to observe. Obviously, there will also have to be follow-up in terms of the consequences. And, as was mentioned earlier, you may need to use both positive and negative consequences.

Contracts should initially be short-term, maybe about two weeks. This allows you to assess their viability and make necessary changes. Consequences should be as immediate as possible; if the reward is too far off, this will seem like forever to some teens and therefore will not motivate them. Realistic, reachable, and desirable goals usually translate into positive motivation.

LIMIT SETTING

When proceeding into action, remember the limits. What is okay and what is not okay? Earlier, we referred to limits with regard to envisioning outcomes and contracts. Sometimes, however, the limits are stated in reference to a relationship. Your relationship with your teen is your trump card. It is valuable, but you cannot play it too often. You can build its value by playing all your other cards (i.e., using your other tools) well. When you play it, you are putting the game on the line.

For example, one teen decided to smoke cigarettes. "Everyone" smoked, he said; besides, he could quit whenever he wanted to. He was not addicted—he simply enjoyed it. His parents "envisioned outcomes" to no avail; he had long since become immune to antismoking propaganda. His parents set up contracts for him, but they really could not monitor his smoking. They needed to say simply and directly how they felt about it and that it was not okay. They told him how upset they were because he was doing something that was hurting him. They loved him, and because of this they could not just sit back and say it was okay or that they realized that there was nothing they could do. They talked to him about it frequently, not in a nagging way but with love and concern. They expressed their disapproval. They talked about their own feelings of worry and sadness. Eventually, this message got through.

These tools reflect ways of bringing Love, Laughter, Limits, and Linkages into our everyday parenting. Part 3 shows you a variety of examples so you can see how one or more of the tools are used together in the context of real parent-teen situations.

■　■　■

Part 3

USING YOUR TOOLS:
SOME EXAMPLES
FOR THE
REAL WORLD

*Observing others' successes can show us new possibilities, expand our
thinking, trigger our creativity. But their experience can never provide models
that will work the same for us. It is good to be inquisitive; it is hopeless to
believe that they have discovered our answers.*

—MARGARET WHEATLEY AND MYRON KELLNER-ROGERS,

A Simpler Way

IN THIS SECTION WE'LL GIVE YOU SOME EXAMPLES AND TELL SOME stories illustrating the use of parenting tools. The general directions (and you know the joke: When all else fails, read the directions) for both you and your teen are to follow the ESP skills from Part 2. You want to do a scan of these skills whenever you are dealing with a problem or making a decision relative to your teen (or to any area of life, for that matter).

For review, you will want to cover these areas:

Evaluate: Know thyself. How are you feeling? Is this a trigger situation for you? If you are feeling stress, be careful. How is your teen feeling? If your teen is feeling stress, be extra careful. What channel is your teen on? Empathize with your children and understand where they are coming from, even if you disagree. We do not always want to do this, especially if we are in conflict with someone. After all, sometimes we feel, "We are right and they are wrong, so what is there to understand?" Well, you cannot tell someone how they should feel, regardless of how strongly you might view those feelings as "wrong." All you can do is show empathy and try to understand. We mean *real* empathy and understanding, not condescending acceptance. Hey, if you love them, try at least to understand them. This does not mean you have to agree with them, but listen very closely to what they are saying. It actually might not be too far from how you are feeling, and there might even be areas of agreement. Remember to try to paraphrase back to check for understanding. Ask at least a couple of open-ended follow-up questions.

While evaluating, *keep your cool and follow the 24-Karat Golden Rule* (to be sung to a rap beat):

> *Don't be a fool.*
> *Keep Calm is your tool.*
> *With anger in check*
> *You won't break your neck.*
> *Talk, don't shout,*
> *The kid's not a lout.*
> *Treat 'em the way you want others to act.*
> *Then they may listen, now that's a fact.*
> *We always say Yo when we run out of lines,*
> *So it's Yo, yo, yo till we run out of rhymes.*

Select: Keep the focus on strengths, ours and our teens'. We can lose perspective and forget to look for the positive in a situation. Try to solve problems. Be clear about your goal and help your teens to be clear about theirs. Plans require some deliberate thought. While your relationships might be emotional and spontaneous, without a plan, quite often no one will get where they want to go.

Proceed: Use your BEST social skills in handling relationships. Remember to model what you want in return. If you communicate in an assertive and open manner, your teen is more likely to respond in kind. Use a contract if other tools are not enough. Do not be afraid to say no and set limits.

When your child is broadcasting on any of the FLASH channels (save Face, Listen to me, looking for an Argument, need Support, need Help), we urge you to put your crystal ball aside and **evaluate** the situation in such a way as to *keep the channels of communication open*. There are three rules to follow:

1. Listen more.
2. Withhold judgment longer.
3. Ask questions that stimulate your teenager's FIG TESPN abilities. Questions like these will serve a useful purpose for you:

F: How are you feeling? Am I right in thinking your voice sounds
___ (for example, a bit anxious) or that you have a ___ look (for
example, worried, eager, nervous)? How do you think I might be
feeling?

I: What would you say is the problem? How do you think the situation looks to me? How might it look if you were me?

G: What do you want to have happen? What's your goal in doing
that? What do you think I want? Do you think I want things to
be negative, angry, or restrictive for you?

T: What are all the different ways you can think of to reach
your goal?

E: If you ___, what might happen? What do you picture happening if you do that? What else?

S: Which of your ideas can you see working out best for you?
Which idea has the best chance of meeting your goal?

P: What will have to happen so you can carry out your idea?
What do you think could possibly go wrong or block your plan?
How can we do this in a calm way without it leading to a blowup?
How are we going to talk to each other?

N: What happened when you tried out your plan? What did you
learn that might help you next time?

We have organized Chapters 7 and 8 with inspiration from the
famous books in the Chicken Soup for the Soul series. Chapter 7
consists mainly of stories—a little dark meat, some vegetables,

maybe a potato. Chapter 8 contains several vignettes and examples of parent-teen dialogues—white meat, a bone or two, some stuffing with gravy, and, of course, dessert. It even features a special section on middle school situations. Remember, don't eat too fast or you'll make yourself sick. You don't have to eat it all in one sitting, either. You can take some home for another day.

Chapter 7

Stories of Teens, Peers, and Parents

THE TALE OF TWO GOALS

Two adolescents, Tom and Jameel, were having difficulty attending school. Both were underachieving, bordering on failure. They had friends and few behavior problems. Tom attended a middle-class high school. His parents were supportive but busy with their own lives. They would drop him off for therapy and be late picking him up. He often missed appointments because they forgot. But in therapy, he was cooperative, if somewhat terse in his responses. Jameel attended an inner-city high school. He lived with his mother, who was involved and supportive. He did not attend counseling, but the school had recommended that he be placed in a special school because of his resistance to learning, and he was undergoing an evaluation. Jameel was also cooperative with adults and polite in his interaction. He just did not like going to school.

In working with both students, we tried to elicit their feelings about school. Both said school was "boring and useless." They denied any particular difficulty with the schoolwork, and both had done adequately in the past. When asked what he wanted to be when he grew up, what his goals in life were, Tom readily said that he wanted to be a police detective. It was clear that Tom had researched this and knew all the details about what detectives did and what their jobs were like. He was quite excited and animated when talking about this, unlike his usual quiet and passive demeanor. However, when asked, Tom admitted that he did not know what kind of education was required to be a detective. Tom was on Channel H and was receptive to help. His assignment in therapy was to research what kind of education was required, which schools provided this, and what kind of grade point average would be necessary to get into those schools. In subsequent sessions, Tom reported that a college education was necessary, that he had picked a first choice, and that he had to have at least a C and preferably a B average to get in. We then discussed how he was going to do this and came up with a plan for waking up in the morning, attending school on time, and completing his schoolwork. Tom did not feel that studying for tests would be necessary to maintain a C to B average, but he was open to future discussion of this.

As a result of this brief intervention, Tom began to get up, go to school, and improve his academic performance. Did he work to his ultimate potential? Probably not. But he did seem happy with his life and his direction in life. He was excited about the future and therefore better able to cope with the present. Tom did not learn to like school, but he learned to view it as a means to an end. His parents also went from being critical to accepting his choices, even though a detective's career was not what they had originally had in mind for their only son.

Jameel also had a specific goal. He wanted to be a professional basketball player. When asked about what this involved, he shrugged. Jameel did not play for his high school team, did not play in a recreation program, and did not even play pickup games with friends. Jameel was encouraged to think about what he could do to reach his goal. He sat silently. When casually asked what he might do if he did not make it to the NBA, as this was certainly an ambitious goal, Jameel had no thoughts. There was nothing else he could even entertain. This story does not have a happy ending. Despite encouragement, Jameel did not develop alternative goals or a plan to achieve his goal of professional basketball. He eventually dropped out of school and has held a variety of minimum-wage jobs.

ESP/FLASH (EVALUATE, SELECT, PROCEED/SAVE FACE, LISTEN TO ME, LOOKING FOR AN ARGUMENT, NEED SUPPORT, NEED HELP) COMMENTARY

Jameel's difficulties represent a problem in our culture. The media can present unrealistic models to children and encourage unattainable goals. It is rare that a television character has an uninteresting job; even when they do, the character is rarely ever shown doing their job. While it might have been possible for Jameel to become a professional basketball player, certainly the odds were stacked against him. In addition, he lacked the motivation necessary to beat the odds. He also evidenced features of depression. When someone is depressed, they tend not to set goals because they lack a positive vision of themselves. Then, unfortunately, this builds on itself, because without goals one tends to achieve less, which makes one more depressed and increases feelings of failure and inadequacy.

The dilemma is, what do we do about Jameel's goal? Do we encourage him, knowing that we are likely setting him up for failure? Or do we steer him away from the goal, toward something that is more realistic and obtainable but perhaps apparently boring? This was quite a frustrating question for his mother. It is necessary to understand that one reason Jameel had such an unrealistic but ambitious goal was to overcompensate for feelings of inadequacy. But just like most defense mechanisms, his unrealistic goal would only reinforce feelings of inadequacy in him.

Jameel needed to be tuned in to Channel S and get some support from significant adults in his life, and maybe even from a basketball coach. It would also be necessary to help Jameel in setting goals by encouraging him to break down his larger goal into smaller, more obtainable units. Through open-ended questioning and the Columbo technique, we would start by helping him see that the way to the NBA was through *playing basketball*. We would then help him set up a goal for himself of joining a league or the school team, if he wanted, and facilitate planning of this. While we worked on this goal and plan, we would also explore other areas of interests and strengths and try to develop goals and plans consistent with those. It is important not to tell an adolescent "No, you can't do that," because one, they will not listen, and two, we want to encourage them, not demoralize them or cause them to blame us for their failure.

THE GIRL WHO DID TOO MUCH

Amie tried to do it all. She was on the soccer team and the yearbook staff and participated in numerous other extracurricular activities. She got good grades. She had friends but not a boyfriend. The problem was that she was not happy. She pushed and pushed herself but never seemed to feel "good enough." Her parents were proud of her but told her she did not have to do all these things. Of course, they expected her to go to a good college and be successful. They were hopeful for a soccer scholarship to get her into a "really good school" and to help defray the costs.

How did Amie feel? Imperfect. No matter how much she tried and achieved, she was never quite content with herself. How did she get this way? Certainly it was not her parents' conscious fault. They were supportive and concerned. However, her parents' feelings of success and achievement were very much caught up with their daughter's. Their pride in her had inadvertently conveyed an expectation of perfection. This was also in part due to Amie's temperament. She was somewhat anxious and driven by nature, a trait she seemed to inherit from her father. Amie was desperately on Channel L (listen to me), but no matter how loud she turned up the volume, her parents did not hear her.

Amie could have continued living this life until maybe, as an adult, she realized she was not happy. Her parents, however, were sensitive enough to her feelings and had the resources to allow her to go to therapy to help her sort things out, although they did not understand what she really needed from them. As a result of being listened to in therapy, Amie chose to continue in all of her activities but did not push herself as much and was able to accept a "good enough" performance. She also learned to be more assertive with her parents, which enabled her to feel more separate from them and not as compelled to please them; but her happiness, more relaxed demeanor, and independence did certainly please them.

ESP/FLASH COMMENTARY

Some adolescents respond to this scenario by outright rebellion or, in the extreme, suicide attempts. This is the fight- (rebellion) or-flight (suicide) response to stress. They can have an attitude that says, "If I can't be what they want me to be, I'll be what they hate—body piercing, sleazy friends, and all." Unfortunately, some teens see no way out. They lack a vision of their future that can be different from their present and internalize their anger rather than externalize it. These kids are at even higher risk, at times, because they do not show outward signs of emotional distress.

However, Amie was a "good kid" who had good values and did want to please her parents. Amie needed to learn to separate and to establish her own identity, focusing on who she was, and not an idealized vision of what she thought her parents wanted her to be. Amie needed permission to not work so hard, to accept that she had limitations and that this was okay. She did not have to do it all, and this did not mean she was a failure. She needed her parents to give her this message not just once, but several times over the course of the year. It was also important that her parents empathized with her and did not just reassure her. Without empathizing, it can sometimes appear to a teen that the parent is not really understanding and is possibly dismissing the teen's feelings.

In addition, her parents needed to sit down with her and help her clarify what it was that she really wanted, to develop a plan to achieve this, and to accept her vision of herself. Fortunately, her parents were able to Keep Calm throughout this, even when they felt criticized. The therapist helped her parents to be aware of their feelings of guilt and sadness concerning their daughter, so that these feelings did not interfere or burden Amie further.

WHEN LIMITS FAIL

Mark was eighteen and, with some friends, was driving his car to a concert, regardless of his parents' feelings. His parents were divorced, and Mark was used to playing one against the other. Both parents happened to agree that he shouldn't drive to the concert, although his father was less vocal about it. Mark said he was going regardless of his parents' limits or concerns. It was his car and he was eighteen. What could they do? They could threaten not to pay for college (an empty threat). They could say he was grounded, but this seemed a little ridiculous, like sending him to his room. His parents felt powerless, and because they were using discipline techniques that worked during childhood, they were right in feeling this way. But they felt they had to do something. Mark was on Channel A: He was looking for an argument to justify doing what he wanted to rather than listening to his parents.

ESP/FLASH COMMENTARY

In this situation, it is necessary for parents to know what they can control and what they cannot. Mark's parents could not control him in this situation. This is extremely frustrating to a parent. Fortunately, his parents were able to Keep Calm and did not blame each other, as they often had in the past. It was important that they understand and validate Mark's feelings (what parent could not identify with wanting to go to a concert with your friends?), but they had to tell Mark clearly and directly, with concern but not anger, how they felt and what their concern was. It was not that they did not trust Mark or that they disliked his friends, but that they felt this was a situation that could lend itself to problems. Yes, they were aware that once he went to college they would not even know about this kind of situation. That was not the point. The point was that this was potentially a problematic or dangerous situation for Mark, and, as his parents, it was their duty to keep him safe. They clearly indicated what the limits were, despite not being able to control the consequences.

Mark ended up driving to the concert with his friends and returned safely. It was important that he registered his parents' disapproval. Hopefully, Mark went with at least a twinge of hesitation and guilt. Maybe next time, Mark would think twice. In any case, this was all his parents could hope for.

THE TALE OF FRIENDS OVER WITHOUT PERMISSION

Jed was thirteen years old. Both his parents worked. He was basically responsible, although his parents perceived him as an underachiever. One day after school, Jed called his mother at work to tell her that he had a friend over and to ask if the friend could stay until after dinner. His mother said this put her in an uncomfortable position because the friend was already there without permission and she did not know how the friend's parents felt about it. Jed assured her that it was okay. Wasn't he being responsible, he asked, by calling her and telling her the friend was over? And, anyway, he was asking for permission now.

ESP/FLASH COMMENTARY

From Jed's point of view, he was being responsible. They were not doing anything wrong or bad, and he did call to ask permission. Hey, what was the big deal? And there was no rule against having friends over. He was on Channel F (saving face). His parents, however, saw it differently. Instead of being influenced by his parents, who Jed knew would not want his friends over without permission, Jed allowed himself to be influenced by his friends. Jed's parents saw this as an example of "peer pressure," in which a peer, rather than they, controls their son's behavior. They trusted their son's judgment when he thought for himself, but they did not trust him when he did not think or when he allowed someone else to think for him.

What was necessary here was for the parents to restate the rules. It was unclear as to what the rule about friends and permission was. Although Jed had maybe exploited this ambiguity, his parents needed to be very clear about this and other house rules so that there could be no more misunderstandings and few loopholes. (All children are lawyers: They look for loopholes, badger witnesses, and object frequently.) Jed's parents also chose not to allow friends over for a week to reinforce Jed's learning of the clarified rule. They also set up a contract with him and made time with friends contingent upon improved school performance.

Jed and his parents also had another talk about peer pressure and the danger associated with allowing your friends to think for you. Jed responded with "Yeah, yeah, I know, I know," but he was told that as his friends would play an increasingly important role in his life, he would face greater and greater peer pressure. His parents helped him solve this problem and come up with solutions to potential situations where he might experience peer pressure.

PORN ON THE INTERNET (WHAT A SURPRISE!)

Peter, age sixteen, was quite computer literate, certainly more so than his mother. He was on-line for hours after school while his mother was at work. He E-mailed, chatted, surfed, and did homework. His mother felt that he was a good kid with good values (despite her ex-husband's influence or lack thereof). They had a close relationship. Peter had some friends, though not many, and did not seem interested in girls yet, which both worried and relieved his mother.

One day, Peter's mother accidentally discovered that Peter had been visiting pornography sites on the Internet. She was shocked. She immediately banned Peter from the Internet. Peter admitted what he had done but said that she could not take the Internet away, since he needed it for school and entertainment. Besides, he asked, what was the big deal about pornography? But he promised he would not visit those sites again. Peter's mother discussed the degradation of women, the deprecating of what should be an act of love, and the immorality of pornography. Peter seemed to get it, and after a week she gave the Internet access back, with child safeguards. Peter complained that this limited his access but said he would put up with it until he had earned his mother's trust or for two weeks, whichever came first.

One week later, Peter's mother discovered that he had bypassed the Internet safeguards and had been at the porno sites again. She was furious and disconnected the computer entirely. Peter was just as angry over her "unjust" consequences. They seemed to be stuck in a battle of wills that was affecting their relationship. Peter's mother was persistent and firm as to the limits. She stated that she understood Peter's curiosity (empathy) but repeated her attitude toward pornography. When Peter eventually saw that he was not going to get his computer back until he had some kind of dialogue with his mother, he began to talk to her more. This time, he really seemed to get it. He was eventually let back on the computer, and his attempts to visit pornography sites seemed to cease.

ESP/FLASH COMMENTARY

Peter's mother evaluated her feelings about pornography prior to talking to Peter. Although she was extremely upset by pornography, she was able to keep her anger and disgust in check. She also understood Peter's feelings of curiosity and the operation of his hormones, so she kept the situation in perspective and knew that to some degree Peter looked at the pornography because it was easily accessible. She did, however, have difficulty coming up with an appropriate course of action (select). She tried to find something that was significant but not too harsh. She was also careful to proceed with good communication and little emotion. Although Peter sometimes wanted to make this into an argument, he also needed to be listened to.

I THINK I'LL KILL MYSELF TO BE HEARD— THEN WE'LL TALK

Janie was a fifteen-year-old girl from an upper-class family. She had many privileges, including private school and regular horseback riding, and she had a full social calendar. However, she felt the angst common among adolescents. Her parents were concerned, but they saw it as her problem. They seemed to have little understanding of her. They were critical of her for things she brought upon herself, like not getting ready on time in the morning, poor grades, and displaying an "attitude." This fueled a lot of yelling and withdrawal on the parts of the parents as well as Janie. Her parents wanted good things for her but did not know how to make them happen. She did not know what she wanted for herself and certainly did not know how to get it.

One night, after a routine fight over something trivial, Janie locked herself in the bathroom and would not come out. Finally, she emerged and announced that she had ingested a bottle of something from the medicine cabinet. She was taken to the emergency room and had her stomach pumped. After an overnight stay and a psychiatric evaluation, she was released and went back home. When asked why she had tried to kill herself, she denied that she had made a suicide attempt and said that she just wanted to be listened to for once. Her action seemed to get her parents' attention and it forced them to take her seriously, at least for a while.

ESP/FLASH COMMENTARY

To start with, it was necessary for Janie's parents to work together. Her parents had to evaluate their own feelings and the goals for the family. Her father worked a great deal and viewed child rearing as his wife's job. His goal was to be the family provider. His wife's goal was to make everything okay at home. However, Janie needed both of her parents, and she needed them to be united in dealing with her, rather than her father withdrawing and her mother feeling alone, overwhelmed, and unsupported. The parents needed time to talk together about their feelings, what they wanted for Janie (and themselves), and how they could make this happen. They then needed to talk with Janie about her feelings and what she wanted and to try to understand her. It was important that she felt listened to by both her parents. They all needed to tune in to Channel L.

Janie was not unreasonable in what she wanted. She was also good at problem solving. For example, one time she wanted to go horseback riding but her mother could not take her. Janie called the stable and made the arrangements and then told her mother that she was calling a taxi, which she would pay for, and that she would try to get a ride home from the stable or would call a friend to pick her up. Rather than praise her responsibility and resourcefulness, her mother nixed the arrangement because she herself had not been involved in the problem solving. This appeared to be a conflict between limit setting and problem definition.

MY TWEEN THINKS SHE'S A TEEN

Prologue: As you may know, "tweens" are the new consumer market. They used to be call "preteens," but this was in the old days, when children still had a childhood. Tweens are the eight- to twelve-year-olds who aspire to be teens. This is their story.

Mary is a typical eleven-year-old. She wears clothes from Limited Too; the Gap is passé. She used to listen to the Backstreet Boys, but they are considered too "Cream of Wheat" now. She rides her bike to the local drugstore to buy makeup with the money she just started to earn baby-sitting. She E-mails and chats and instant messages with abandon, because talking to her friends in school all day just is not enough. According to Mary, her parents don't get it. They keep telling her to do her work, go to bed before 11:00 P.M., spend time with her relatives, and be decent to people who are not cool.

Mary does not consider herself a child. She wants to grow up in the worst way, and that is sometimes the problem: She *does* grow up in the worst way. She does not really understand what it means to be a teenager. And, of course, she has the emotional needs of an eleven-year-old. She needs to save face with her peers and wants to be listened to, but at the same time she provokes arguments because of all of her own conflicting feelings. What she needs most is support through this difficult time in her life and help in navigating the waters of early adolescence.

ESP/FLASH COMMENTARY

These are hard times for this age group. They are being exposed to values and pressures from all sides, but especially from the unfiltered media. Television gives her values and tells her how to be accepted by others. Her peers exaggerate their own rebellious behavior and put pressure on her to keep up in order to be cool. The Internet does not actually bring her closer to others but allows her to hide behind the anonymity of her screen name. She is not learning life skills because she is not playing; she is pretending to be an adult.

What can her parents do for her? First, they can understand the pressures she is under both at school and socially. Kids today are learning more and at a faster rate. They have to keep up. Schools are focused on test scores, not children. Mary faces social pressures at her age that her parents never dreamed of. She has access to information her parents are still embarrassed by.

Her parents need to help her by listening carefully (Channel L). Mary does not really want to grow up so fast. Many times she is hesitant about what she is doing but is afraid to let others know her doubts; after all, everyone else can handle it. Her parents then need to validate her feelings and help her solve problems. What does she really want? What would happen if she did something different from her friends—would they really drop her? And her parents must not hesitate to set firm limits, out of love. She will seem to rebel, but she mostly will be grateful because, at some level, she knows that her parents' decisions are better than her peers' decisions. Giving her appropriate linkages to positive role models and responsibilities is also important. For many tweens, when their parents take their religious training seriously, it is a source of positive values.

NO MONEY, NO COLLEGE

Randy was always told that if he worked hard, he could go to any college he wanted. This was before his parents' divorce, which occurred during his last year of high school. Randy kept up his part of the deal and graduated near the top of his class and was accepted into an Ivy League school. Then the bottom dropped out of his life. In the middle of his freshman year, he was told that his parents could no longer afford tuition. He could go to a state school or he was on his own.

Randy was devastated. Everything he had worked for his whole life was gone. Everything his parents had said was important was suddenly expendable. Understandably, Randy became depressed. What did he have? Nothing, he thought.

ESP/FLASH COMMENTARY

Randy had the maturity and courage to seek help. In therapy, he was listened to and empathized with. He was reminded of his strengths of personality, intelligence, and the capacity for hard work. He was refocused on his goal, which was to get back into school, with the first step being to visit the financial aid office and see what options he had.

He felt abandoned by his parents, which in a sense was true.

His parents did not do well in their awareness of his feelings and in their problem solving. Rather than *telling* Randy their solution, they could have *included him in problem solving*. Unfortunately, his parents were not using their BEST skills when talking with him and they tended to either be passive, i.e., neglect to tell him what was going on, or become angry with him when he did not seem to understand their perspective. These are the kinds of things that, over the years, can drive a wedge between children and their parents that can be very hard to dislodge.

DO WHAT I SAY, IT'S FOR YOUR OWN GOOD

Jim, age sixteen, did not always use good judgment. He got into a variety of problems, some serious, some minor. He was on probation for driving his parents' car drunk and without a license. He had academic difficulties because of his lack of effort and organization but was attending a vocational high school, which he enjoyed more and where he did better in his applied subject areas. He had loving and concerned parents who were very worried about his ability to become independent. They would do anything for him.

Jim often argued with his parents (Channel A). He frequently rebelled against their control, either overtly by disobeying them or covertly by lying to them. As a result of Jim's past mistakes, his parents tried to control everything he did. They told him when to study, what he needed to do for school, what he was not doing at home, what they thought he should be doing with his free time, and so on. Jim sometimes listened, which seemed to reinforce his parents' advice-giving role, but he was caught in an adolescent no-man's-land. He did not really take his parents seriously and was not really independent. Although this could describe most adolescents, Jim's predicament was particularly extreme, in that his relationships with his parents were as problematic as his independent actions. He rejected his parents but could not be independent.

ESP/FLASH COMMENTARY

Understandably, Jim's parents were not very positive about him. They viewed him and almost everything he did negatively, which was not surprising, given his history. Their lives were filled with trigger situations, from waking him up in the morning to telling him to go to bed at night. His parents were in a constant state of stress. In some ways, Jim's parents were too empathic; they felt all of Jim's pain and tried to do something about all of it. The pressure of trying to make everything better all the time threw the balance of Love, Laughter, and Limits way off.

Jim's parents needed to focus on their goal, which was to foster independence. They thought that by trying to control him they would be teaching him how to live correctly. They were afraid to step back and allow him to make his own mistakes because of the severity of the consequences Jim had already experienced. In order to step back and allow Jim to solve his own problems, they had to use their own Keep Calm skills a great deal. Contracting with him was effective, as long as they were willing to allow him to occasionally not meet with their expectations—and not rescue him by making excuses. Overall, they needed to solve the problem of what to do, because trying to "control" him was not working. Things improved once they realized that nothing would work in the immediate future. Most important was that Jim's parents maintain a relationship with him by letting him know that they would be tuned in to the support and help channels when *he* was ready; this way they wouldn't continually try to tune him in to those stations.

IT'S MY ROOM AND YOU KEEP OUT: WHAT ARE THE LIMITS TO PRIVACY?

Maggie, age thirteen, resented her parents' intrusions into her life. She liked to come home, go to her room, and lock the door. She had her own phone, television, and computer in her room.

She had two younger siblings, who always "bothered" her, she said, and that's why she had to lock her door. Her parents respected her privacy but knew very little about what she did in her room. She did okay in school, and her teachers never indicated a problem. Her parents did not really know her friends but suspected that there was a boy she liked, although they did not know who. Sometimes her parents wondered if there was a problem, but there were no indications, so they assumed everything was okay. They attributed her withdrawal from the family to normal teenage behavior. Was this a problem waiting to happen, or was this "normal"?

ESP/FLASH COMMENTARY

"Keep your child safe" is the first rule of parenting. Maggie's parents could not fully answer the question "Do you know what your child is doing?" They assumed she was safe, but they did not really know. Her parents were right in understanding that privacy was a strong need in adolescence, but what were the limits to privacy? To quote Ronald Reagan about his approach to dealing with those he wanted to befriend but also worried about, "Trust but verify"; that is, trust that her need for privacy is not masking serious problems but verify that this is the case.

Maggie's parents do need to know more about her. They need to give her the opportunity to let them listen to her. That is easier said than done, of course. What might work? They could spend more time talking with her, using open-ended, probing questions, as we mentioned earlier. An occasional family meeting, where everyone sits down to discuss and negotiate the limits of privacy, would be helpful. If she refuses to meet, they shouldn't panic: They should just take the door off her room. (As the parents, you can do this. It is *your* door!) She will then very quickly agree to meet, and as often as you like.

Remember, teens feel strongly about privacy even when there is really nothing to hide; it is the principle. Maggie's parents can help her save face by reaching a reasonable compromise. Of course, sometimes teens will emphasize privacy because they do have something to hide that they feel you would disapprove of. Keep in mind Shakespeare's line, "The lady doth protest too much"—adjusted for your child's gender, of course—when trying to assess your teen's truthfulness. In addition, never underestimate the power of denial. You, too, may be subject to this. No one wants to believe bad things about their children.

Above all, there needs to be an atmosphere of openness. Teens who feel criticized are less likely to engage in open and honest discussion. Don't take it personally if your teen lies to you. It is not uncommon, and it may be a way of promoting independence. If you overreact to your teens' dishonesty, they will be less likely to open up to you in the future; nevertheless, you should be clear as to what the limits are. (And you know how difficult the situation is when we invoke both Shakespeare and Ronald Reagan as sources of parenting advice!)

THE PART-TIME JOB

DAD: With all the time on your hands, don't you think you should be looking for a part-time job?

SON: Well, Dad, you know, studies have shown that teens engaged in part-time employment do not achieve as high a grade point average. I really want to be focused on school right now.

DAD: That's great, except you aren't focused on school. I see you spending a lot of time with your friends and listening to music.

SON: You just don't get it. It isn't easy going to school and dealing with everything I have to deal with. I need downtime. I'm not a workaholic like you. Just because you are so fixated on money doesn't mean I have to be. You are never home anyway.

DAD: You seem to enjoy the fruits of my labor, even though you don't appreciate it much.

ESP/FLASH COMMENTARY

Did you see the sparks flying? This is a volatile situation. Both father and son are upset and not empathizing or understanding each other's point of view. It would be important at this point for the father to initiate some empathy and paraphrasing. For example:

SON: You just don't get it. It isn't easy going to school and dealing with everything I have to deal with. I need downtime. I'm not a workaholic like you. Just because you are so fixated on money doesn't mean I have to be. You are never home anyway.

DAD (paraphrasing): I understand that you find school stressful. It sounds like other things are more important to you than work right now. I want you to know that I am also frustrated by my work schedule sometimes and do feel badly about not being home.

The father might also clarify why he wants his son to work. The father wants him to work not because he views his son as lazy, which is a negative way of seeing the situation, but because he wants him to learn to be more responsible. The father also believes that work experience will teach his son important life skills, such as time and money management. The father might convey this as:

DAD: It isn't the money that is important here. Sometimes through work you learn important skills that aren't taught in school and you find out things about yourself you didn't know. You get a sense of what you are really capable of. Also, I think working can give you a taste of the real world and help you decide what you want to be.

The son may or not be receptive to hearing these things, but the father will have a better chance of being heard. When the father models understanding and empathy, he invites the son to listen to him more, rather than inciting defensiveness and anger on the son's part. The father cannot do any of this, however, if he does not remember to Keep Calm.

ADDICTION TO THE INTERNET AND VIDEO GAMES

Like many teens, Bill was into the computer. It was something he was good at and enjoyed. He had a computer in his room with Internet access. He played games on the computer, chatted, E-mailed, and occasionally did some homework. He looked forward to coming home and going on-line. Bill did not get into any trouble at school, and he earned fairly good grades. His parents did not see anything wrong with the long amount of time he spent in his room on the computer. He was not doing anything "bad," and he had many Internet friends. He did not converse much with his parents or go out that often. His parents attributed this to "being a teenager."

ESP/FLASH COMMENTARY

It could be argued that Bill is truly a child of the twenty-first century. He grew up with the computer, is comfortable with it, and can utilize it to its full potential for academic, economic, entertainment, and social purposes. Aside from food and shelter, the computer provides all he really needs in life.

However, is this really true? Is Bill really finding fulfillment through his computer? One extensive study of Internet use showed that the more people used the Internet, the more lonely and depressed they became. In addition, Bill was not learning or practicing real social skills. Typing to someone on a keyboard is not the same as interacting with them in person. What is lost is the emotional component, the expression of empathy, which is conveyed through all the nonverbal signals of BEST that are not available via a screen. Researchers are beginning to recognize that what is important to people is not that their environments are "high-tech" but that they are "high-touch."

What should Bill's parents do? Is there really a problem? Bill is happy and would be resistant to any attempts to take away his access to the world. Most parents would not view this situation as abnormal or problematic, especially those parents who also live their lives on-line. The question is really one of balance. Of course Bill should continue to be allowed to use his computer, but he also needs real relationships. His parents need to encourage social activities, such as extracurricular school clubs, sports, a religious youth group, or even a computer club where members meet in person, not in cyberspace. Bill certainly might oppose his parents' meddling in his life, but they could then use the computer as a motivation. His use of the computer could be tied to his participation in social activities. This should be explained to him not as a punishment (even if he interprets it this way) but as a parental duty to ensure his well-rounded development, like forcing him to eat vegetables and write thank-you notes to relatives who send gifts.

So don't go along with the delusion that the computer world is enough. Set limits on computer use, take the heat from this decision if it comes, and make sure your teenagers have some good old-fashioned, nonlogical, nonlinear human interactions!

IS THERE A THIRTEEN-YEAR-OLD BOY WITH AN ANNOYING TEN-YEAR-OLD BROTHER?

Two brothers used to be best friends, but since the older one became a teenager, he wants nothing to do with his younger brother. His brother is crushed by this and annoys his older brother just to get some attention. What is a parent to do?

ESP/FLASH COMMENTARY

First of all, this pattern is not unusual. Many people would consider you lucky to have had even one or two years of positive sibling relationships. Be assured that the foundation for a good relationship has already been formed and they will likely come back to it. It is important that you accept and empathize with the feelings of both sons in such situations. Explain to both that this is normal and it is not a rejection of either one. Help them to empathize with each other. Then help them decide on their goals. What does each one want? The younger child probably wants to play with his older brother. It is important for him to see that annoying his older brother is not getting him what he wants. The older brother may want his space. Ignoring his younger brother is not getting him what he wants either, because the more he ignores him, the more annoying he becomes. It would be useful to have both boys solve this problem together at a family meeting after a statement of their goals. How can they each get more of what they want and less of what they don't want? This is a question that, with a little parental guidance, can lead to a solution that will give both children self-respect for having had the competencies to deal with some of their issues on their own.

Chapter 8

Parent-Teen Vignettes and Conversations

*Help Your Early Adolescents Deal
with Stress and Help Your Older Teens
Deal with Sex, Love, and Relationships*

This chapter has two sections. The first deals with middle schoolers, possibly the most misunderstood group in the teenage years. We will show you some of the intense stress they feel during this period, why they do, and how your emotionally intelligent conversations with them can lower their stress and raise their E.Q. The second section is something we call Ben and Jerry's for the Teenage Hole. The hole is the empty feeling older teenagers get when their relationships go badly and they are not sure what to do about their love lives…which is most of the time. Chicken soup is good, but it passes through the system too quickly. Ben and Jerry's plugs up the holes, soothes the wounds, and comes in enough varieties to appeal to nearly everyone. And there is always frozen yogurt, sorbet, and, if all else fails, Lactaid.

THE MIDDLE SCHOOL TRANSITION
IS HARDER THAN YOU THINK

When we discussed developmental issues earlier, we certainly addressed the topic of transitions. There are a number of them in adolescence, and each one represents a sort of "rite of passage." One of our favorite books on this topic is *Crossroads: The Quest for Contemporary Rights of Passage* (Louise Mahdi, Nancy Christopher, and Michael Meade, Open Court Press, 1996); it provides numerous examples of how different cultures and groups mark the transitions of adolescence. Many of these transitions are spiritual or faith-based in nature, such as Bar and Bat Mitzvahs and Confirmation. We strongly advocate the need to handle these sensitive and important situations with emotional intelligence.

Here we want to address a transition that does not get the attention is deserves: the transition to middle school. In different communities, it can occur after fifth, sixth, or even seventh grade; occasionally, it will occur after fourth grade. And some of us are from schools that went from kindergarten through grade eight, which saved us this transition and brought us directly into high school.

Interestingly, some researchers would say that those who avoid middle school are better off. Why is that?

1. The transition to middle school marks a time of increased referrals to mental-health services.

2. The events of puberty combine with changes in cognitive and social development to make the middle school transition quite complex. Lots of things are happening at once, more than during any other general school-related transition.

3. The change from an elementary to a middle school is primarily a qualitative change; the change from middle to high school is mostly a quantitative change.

4. Rates of problems with smoking, alcohol, drugs, and violence, which appear to peak in high school, really have their start in middle school. The same is true with dropping out of school and disaffection.

5. Girls suffer particular damage to their self-esteem and seem to lose interest and confidence in math and science subject areas and careers, largely due to social pressures they experience during the middle school years.

For these reasons, we want to provide a focus on some different aspects of the middle school experience to help you prevent or reduce some of the negatives that can result during that time.

To start with, let's take a look at what research indicates are the critical "tasks" that middle school students must get used to during the transition. As you read about them, think about which ones might present small, medium, or large problems for your middle school child. It's also useful for you to reflect on the extent to which these might have been problems for your high school–aged child, and perhaps even for you, if you attended a middle school:

Logistics of the New Building and Routine
Getting lost and not being able to find your way around the school
Forgetting your locker combination
Having the school be farther away from your home
Buying new notebooks
Eating in a larger cafeteria
Leaving the wrong books and supplies in your locker and forgetting to bring the right books and supplies to class

Increased Academic Demands
Having a tough teacher
Having to do harder schoolwork
Getting too much homework
Teachers expecting too much of you

Dealing with Conflict, Authority Figures, and Older Students
Having an argument with a teacher
Being sent to the vice principal's office
Getting into fights
Kids trying to talk you into doing things you don't want to do
Getting things stolen from you
Being bothered by older kids
Not getting along with all your different teachers

Peer Relationships
Not seeing your friends from elementary school enough
Having trouble making new friends

Wishing you were in a better reading group
Other kids teasing you
Not being in the "in" group
Kids seeing you in the locker room and making fun of you
Dating

Pressures to Get Involved in Substance Use
Drinking beer, wine, or liquor
Taking drugs
Smoking cigarettes

These five areas cover concerns found among middle school children not only throughout the United States but wherever there is a middle school system of education. Many trips to the school nurse and no small number of phantom ailment–related absences are caused by the problems of teens trying to cope with these tasks and the strong feelings they engender.

For the various examples that follow, then, please keep in mind how students' likely experiences in middle school, along with the developmental issues noted earlier, add to their stress and make it harder than we might think for them to cope.

PEER PRESSURE IN THE MIDDLE SCHOOL: CIGARETTE SMOKING

We don't know an adolescent who has not come in contact with smoking, and the majority have had contact with alcohol use. Many also know about drug use among their peers. These are difficult and complex issues. Also, research data suggests that parents cannot use the same approach to all three. Since smoking is seen as a "gateway" to other substance use, let's focus on how to prevent it. This is an issue of limits…being clear about our values and point of view and then taking appropriate steps with our teens.

First, look at yourself and your family. Who smokes? What is your teenager's understanding of this? We would be lying if we said you can get away with "Do as I say, not as I do" in this matter. Consider strongly making your house a smoke-free zone and asking that guests also follow this rule. The next step is to make your car a smoke-free zone. Now, at least, you are making a solid value statement. A further value statement is when you and other smoking relatives actively and visibly engage in trying to stop the habit.

Second, we have to deal realistically with the peer pressure to smoke (or use other drugs) your kids might experience. Be aware that teenagers overestimate the number of their peers who smoke, drink, do drugs, or, for that matter, are involved in sex; peer pressure appears stronger than it really is. Further, when you talk to teenagers individually, they are far less positive about such experiences than they are in a group setting. Many teens recognize the downsides of smoking, alcohol, and drug use.

Our task as parents is twofold. We want to provide Love, Laughter, and Linkages that will make smoking and the like difficult to engage in. If our kids have positive, nonsmoking peer groups where they make contributions and use their talents constructively, they are much less likely to seek out smoke-friendly peer groups and contexts. Parents sometimes need to join together and look at their middle and high schools' policies and procedures related to smoking. For example, purchasing cigarettes is illegal in many communities if children are under age eighteen. In the vicinity of many schools, even if not technically on their property, one can see students smoking. Where did they get these cigarettes? Either from parents, which the law does permit in all cases we are aware of, or from stores or machines, which is illegal.

We also encourage parents who want their teenagers to grow up healthy (and educators who want the same thing for their students) to be active in working together with school nurses, the police, local businesses, and other local groups to find ways to confront teens who are below the legal age for cigarette purchases. They need to be asked, "Where did you get these?" If they say from a certain business, then follow-up with that store is essential. If they say from their parents, then we suggest that a form of "summons" be given to those parents, stating something like the following:

Dear Parent/Guardian:

On ___ (date), your teenager was observed smoking in public. We have been informed that you are the source of the cigarettes your child is smoking. We need to confirm this, as the purchase of cigarettes by children below the age of ___ is illegal in our community. Please indicate below which of the following is the case and return this summons to ___ by ___. If we do not get this back, we will contact your teenager again and be in direct touch with you. Thank you.

___ I provide my child's cigarettes and I am aware of the dangers of smoking. He/she has my approval.
___ I do not provide my child's cigarettes and would like to work with you to find out the source and see that this does not continue.
___ I would like to be contacted for further information about this.

We recognize that we are taking an extreme position and that refinement of this approach, which we have urged informally in different situations, requires legal examination to ensure that everyone's legal rights are being preserved. But we feel that one has a moral right to protect children from habits—in this case, addictions—that are dangerous to their health and are in no way positive contributors to their growth and future.

While we focus here on cigarette smoking, alcohol and/or drugs could be added or even substituted in what follows. To start things off, try to use a natural situation. These include seeing a billboard advertising cigarettes or just witnessing someone else smoking. For example, imagine that you are in a fast-food hamburger restaurant with your thirteen-year-old, eighth-grade son. Some folks are smoking cigarettes in one section of the restaurant. As you sit down to eat, you have the following dialogue:

DAD: Do a lot of the kids at school smoke, Matthew?
MATTHEW: What do you mean?

DAD: Cigarettes.

MATTHEW: (Pause.) Yeah, some do.

DAD: Any of your friends?

MATTHEW: Not really.

DAD: What have you decided to do?

MATTHEW: What do you mean?

DAD: I mean if someone offers you a cigarette.

MATTHEW: What difference does it make, you and Mom wouldn't let me, even if I wanted to.

DAD: Well, yes...but we really don't know what you think about it. We were wondering how you'd respond if there was any pressure at school to smoke.

MATTHEW: You sure you want to talk about this?

DAD: Yes.

MATTHEW: Well, I would probably say no.

DAD: Uh...anything else?

MATTHEW: I could say I don't want to get into trouble.

DAD: What if it's your best friend?

MATTHEW: Well, I could just say it's bad for you and walk away.

DAD: Well, those all sound like good ideas. Could we go over them again?

MATTHEW: Say no...say I don't want to get into trouble...say it's bad for your health and just walk away.

DAD: Well, what is the best choice?

MATTHEW: A little of each. I'd say no, that it was bad for your health, and then I'd leave.

DAD: All good ideas...I'm glad that we talked.

MATTHEW (smiling): Well, Dad, I'm glad you feel better. I will send you a bill tomorrow. I hope I am listed as a provider in your health plan. Now can we eat finally?

A LACK-OF-PROGRESS REPORT COMES HOME FROM MIDDLE SCHOOL

Hari Kumar is an eighth-grade student in a middle school. He has never gotten a failing grade or even a bad comment from school.

But his run of good luck is over—he just got a progress report that says he is failing in social studies as of the middle of the marking period. Watch how his dad uses feelings, establishes empathy, and moves toward constructive action. He is able to put aside his own disappointments and focus more on how his child is feeling:

HARI (waiting until supper before he tells his parents about the progress report): Mom and Dad, there is something you have to sign.

MRS. KUMAR: Yes, Hari, what is it?

HARI: Oh, it's just a progress report from school.

MR. KUMAR: That sounds interesting. What is the progress about?

HARI: Well, a...a...here. (Hari bows his head and hands the paper to his dad.)

MR. KUMAR (looks at the report and frowns): Progress—how can they call this a progress report—sounds like no progress to me! Well, son, what about this?

MRS. KUMAR: Yes, Hari. Did you know that you were failing in social studies?

HARI: Well, sorta. There was this big test and I got a sixty-five. That really messed up my grade. I have thought about what I can do. I'm going to study very hard for the next test.

MR. KUMAR (smiling): I'm glad to hear that you're thinking about what you can do to improve your grade. What other things are you graded on in social studies?

HARI: Oh, we have group projects and the teacher grades us on class participation...

MR. KUMAR: It sounds like you know what areas to work on to bring up your grade. Would you like some help in reviewing the material before your next test?

HARI: Thanks, Dad. But I think I can do it. I thought you would be angry.

MR. KUMAR: Well, I was shocked and curious, really. I feel a little better now because you say you're planning on working harder. And if your work is better but your grades are not, we can talk to the school. Besides, you are doing well in everything else!

ESP/FLASH (EVALUATE, SELECT, PROCEED/SAVE FACE, LISTEN TO ME, LOOKING FOR AN ARGUMENT, NEED SUPPORT, NEED HELP) COMMENTARY

Handling academic difficulty can be tough for students, teachers, and parents as well. But raising an emotionally intelligent teenager requires you to keep your *child's* head and heart in focus and not let your own feelings hijack you into an extreme reaction. Hari's dread was not matched by his parents' dread, and it's a good thing—the mix could have been explosive! Instead, his parents put aside their shock and were able to focus on supporting Hari. His parents left open the idea of having a conference with the social studies teacher to find out more about expectations for classroom participation and the material being covered. Perhaps Hari is reluctant to admit to difficulty or ask for assistance. It is also possible that the teacher has a grading procedure that is tougher than Hari's previous classes have offered. Parents need to keep tuned to their children's needs for support and help through difficult situations as well as through comfortable ones.

POOR EYESIGHT, GREAT VISION: JACQUI HAS HER GOALS IN FOCUS AND FIG TESPN AT HER SIDE

Jacqui is one of several students at Pacheco Middle School who has poor eyesight. Although she is not blind, she must sit in the front of her classes, and sometimes she has trouble getting around the school without bumping into people or objects. Jacqui takes the bus to school and sits in the front, right behind the driver, so she doesn't have to walk so much in the narrow aisles. But the bus ride is a time when some of her schoolmates tease her. They say things like, "Hey, Four Eyes!" "Watch out you don't trip on your feet!" and "Look out for that thing on the floor—watch out!"

Some of Jacqui's most uncomfortable feelings emerge on the bus ride home, during which she hears everyone talk about what they are going to do that day. It's hard for Jacqui to be involved in bicycling, shopping, walking around in the mall, playing ball, even watching television without her special set. Not surprisingly, Jacqui feels left out.

But Jacqui does well in school. She spends a lot of time reading, working with the computer, and studying. She learns things quickly. Jacqui also can sing exceptionally well. Her teachers and parents give her much praise, and she has learned to accept that praise and enjoy it.

Here is an example of a not unusual Thursday when Jacqui has just arrived home from school. Her mother notices some signs that Jacqui is particularly upset:

MOTHER: Jacqui, it looks like the bus ride was pretty rough.

JACQUI: No, not much worse than usual. Cathy and Teri were calling me names like "teacher's pet" and "brainy"; even Maryanne called me something. But I'm not too upset at that.

MOTHER: Well, your voice is shaking a little—something must be bothering you.

JACQUI: I want to go to my room and think, Mom. I don't want to talk now.

In her room, Jacqui tries to understand why she is so upset. She has learned the value of ESP and uses it to help her cope. She is aware of feeling upset, but she cannot identify anything different that happened on the bus. She felt upset when she was teased, but she feels wonderful about her schoolwork and her singing projects. "What's the problem?" she asks herself. And then she puts her feelings into words in a way that feels right. It has to do with hearing the other students' point of view and reflecting on the differences. "I'm upset because I'm alone so much. No kids hear my singing. No one even asks for my help with homework. My problem is that I'm lonely!" Then a smile appears on her face as she walks out the door. She had evaluated her situation and is now ready to select a way to respond to it: "My goal is that I make some friends who will share things I like to do."

Her mother takes one look at Jacqui and realizes that the tension and stress she brought into the house has almost vanished. "Jacqui, you seem so much more relaxed." "Yeah, I guess so." "Where are you going?" "I'm checking my assignments for the week to see when I can invite some friends over after school."

ESP/FLASH COMMENTARY

Jacqui was broadcasting her upset but was also clear that she wanted support but not help. This example is an illustration of the preventive approach we believe in so strongly. Middle school kids have a lot to cope with. The time to build their skills is as early as possible. Her mother did not wait until Jacqui was teased beyond endurance; starting in elementary school, she spent a great deal of time building her own and her daughter's skills in emotional intelligence. While Jacqui's level of self-awareness is unusual for a middle school–aged child, it is not developmentally exceptional. It's just that until problems are seriously apparent, we too rarely value the time it takes to teach the life skills and social and emotional competencies children will need.

Jacqui had the FIG TESPN strategy to use when she was upset. She had learned that once she looked at her situation and feelings, put her problem into words, and decided on a goal, she felt relief. She could then take whatever action might be necessary.

In the example above, Jacqui mentions Maryanne. Working in small communities sometimes lets us see different sides of a problem. Here is how the bus rides look from someone else's point of view.

STRONG FEELINGS CAN BE OVERWHELMING: MARYANNE NEEDS A STRATEGY FOR KEEPING HER GOALS IN FOCUS

"I hate the bus rides to and from middle school," thinks Maryanne. "People throw things out the window, take each other's books and hats, and call other people names." Maryanne wishes she could just be invisible and sit in her seat without being noticed. Most of the time, she actually can do this. She sits down low and stares in front of her. But every so often, Cathy gets her involved in something terrible.

"Hey, Maryanne. What do you think of Four Eyes?" "What?" Maryanne feels her heart pounding. "Everybody in this row has to say two things to Four Eyes or else their books are going out the window," says Cathy. "And it's your turn!" Maryanne's heart keeps pounding. Her throat is dry. Teri says, "C'mon, Maryanne. It's your turn. It's your turn." "Open the window," says Cathy. It has never been this bad before, thinks Maryanne. "Where'd you get those ugly glasses?" screams Maryanne to Jacqui. "They make your eyes look like peas," she adds. Everyone laughs and laughs. She is congratulated so much, she finds herself smiling!

At home Maryanne starts to feel uneasy. She can't quite figure out why. "It's wrong to call her names. But how could I let them throw my books out? Jacqui's nice, though. She once helped me with a math problem. And I made fun of her glasses! But Cathy and Teri sure were proud of me. They'll probably let me eat lunch with them. Maybe they'll leave me alone on the bus. But what if they bother me more? Jacqui did look surprised when I yelled at her. What if Mrs. Morgan finds out? She thinks I'm nice, and pretty smart!"

Maryanne's heart again begins to pound and her mouth gets dry. She gets a soda from the refrigerator and puts on her favorite radio station, loud. Pretty soon, she is repeating some lyrics and isn't noticing her heart, mouth, or her problem anymore.

ESP/FLASH COMMENTARY

Middle school–aged students, struggling to figure out who they are and who they are going to become, have to deal with many, often competing social and emotional forces. Both Maryanne and Jacqui experienced stress. And a frequent cause of stress is *goal confusion*. Goal confusion occurs when we have too many conflicting goals, or our goals are too vague to give us a clear direction. Goal confusion can also occur when we do not have goals, such as in persons who seem to just "go with the flow" and do not follow a consistent direction that is *theirs*. Read back through the examples for both girls and notice the different goals that each is trying to sort through. Then read on!

Let's look first at Jacqui. She had several major choices: 1) get people to stop teasing her, 2) be like "everyone else," 3) not get upset by the teasing, and 4) develop positive, sharing friendships. Jacqui kept thinking about her different feelings and possible ways to put her problem into words until she found one that seemed right to her. Somewhere along the way, Jacqui learned how to focus on her uncomfortable feelings and not instantly try to get rid of them or distract herself. She learned that by evaluating situations and feelings and putting them into words, she could "see" how they related to selecting a goal. It was after finding a genuine goal and then taking the appropriate action that she truly felt relief from her stress.

Maryanne is in a different place. She has not been helped to step back and evaluate her experiences on the bus. Each day is a day of dread. The goal, if there is one, is simply to get through it. But what does Maryanne really want to have happen? Does she want to be liked by Cathy and Teri? To keep her books on the bus? To "do unto others"? To make sure her teacher thinks well of her? To be nice to Jacqui? To be left alone?

When children, especially early adolescents, don't have a strategy for managing their strong emotions, they do what many sufferers of goal confusion do—avoid the stress by drowning it out. Maryanne used music, but sometimes music is not "strong" enough. Then what? That's when we are more likely to see involvement in such dangerous strategies as alcohol use, delinquent acts, or drug involvement.

Another difference in the two examples is the role of a parent. Like most children of middle school age (and especially boys), Jacqui and Maryanne tend to keep to themselves when problems arise. They sometimes feel ashamed. They also feel, because of developmental issues noted earlier, that their problems are far more momentous than they are in reality. In Jacqui's home, her mom is highly involved. She is not necessarily intrusive, but she is on top of things. She pays careful attention to Jacqui's usual moods and is especially alert to nonverbal signs of changes.

Maryanne's family tends to give her too much distance. They don't want to upset her or cause conflicts. They notice things but then take all their cues from Maryanne. At this point, they have stopped tuning in to her broadcast channels and might not hear L (listen to me) and H (I need help) when the signals are being sent.

Let's be clear here: This is not about parents necessarily being home when their kids return from school. But it *is* about Love and Linkages. Children of middle school age still need to be with people who are sensitive to their feelings and who can help them with difficulties they are experiencing—difficulties that we know, developmentally, are expected. Often by the time we get to see our kids, they have found a way to alleviate their stress; we won't know much about it unless we probe and our children are able to reflect on and talk about their feelings.

One sign to be alert for: When little provocations get big emotional reactions, that is often a clue that our kids have unresolved emotional issues lurking. It takes a lot of emotional energy to hide a stressful situation that continues to "work" on us. And so when a small, new provocation comes along, the overreaction is a broadcast by our kids that we need to attend to. Of course, they will not necessarily be receptive, and we have to be smart about when we follow up. But we cannot allow ourselves to overlook such signals just because we are so exhausted and stressed ourselves that we don't know how we would manage if we found out for sure that there was a problem we had to deal with.

To close these thoughts, here is an example of what we mean and how it might be handled well:

MOM: Let's get the table cleared off and start studying.
TOMMY: Will you just shut up already? How many times do you have to say things to me? And I already did a lot of studying.

Mom has two big tasks: to resist the urge to "counterattack," and to regroup and find a way to address the issue when she will have a chance of success. Here is one strategy we have seen work often:

MOM (speaking softly and calmly, while clenching her fists and jaw): I don't appreciate being spoken to in that way. Please take care of what I asked. Later on, I want to talk to you about a few things.

If Tommy replies—a fifty-fifty chance—Mom needs to repeat herself, and even more calmly, if at all possible. What is Mom doing here? First of all, anger often plays off anger. Health educator Vicki Poedubicky likens it to Newton's third law: For every action, there is an equal and opposite reaction. Anger brings forth anger. So Mom is trying to break the cycle and give her son less to respond to, less fuel for the fire. Second, Mom is letting Tommy know that they will talk later. This begins to help him prepare for sharing what is happening. He might not be doing so at a conscious level. It often happens that Mom's words bring about a form of nonverbal relief, as if the child is saying: "Whew, I have been holding this in for so long. I feel like I am going to explode sometimes. But I can't let it out myself. I am too scared, ashamed, confused. But Mom is going to talk to me about it. She either must know or else she suspects. Either way, she will find out and maybe she can help me, or at least I won't feel so bad."

Set the wheels in motion. Remember to follow up. Bring your

tools from Part 2 with you, especially the Columbo technique and active listening. Don't expect success, but don't give up either. Your child's room, your child's feelings, and your child's raw anger can all seem like the narrow bridge we mentioned earlier. You must proceed without fear and keep going until you arrive at your destination.

With this in mind, here is one way Mom might follow up on the previous situation:

MOM: Tommy, remember earlier when I asked you to start studying and you seemed to get very angry? I was just wondering, what was going on?

TOM: Nothing. I just hate it when you tell me to do stuff all the time.

MOM: I'm not sure I understand. You don't want my help studying?

TOM: No, well, yeah, but when I want it.

MOM: I can understand that. But you seemed to be really angry. Is anything bothering you?

TOM: Why do you always think something is bothering me? You read too many of those *Six Steps to a Perfect Child* books.

MOM: That's a good title—I'll have to use it for my memoirs. Seriously, is there anything bothering you?

TOM: I'm not doing that well in science.

MOM (containing her disappointment): Oh. Is that why you got so upset when we started talking about homework?

TOM: Maybe.

MOM: Please let me know if there's anything I can do to help. But also, please remember that things go a lot better if you can tell me what's going on rather than just showing me there is a problem by yelling at me. Do you want to talk about science now?

SIBLING SQUABBLE

Jonny and Roger, ages nine and fourteen, start arguing and pushing each other. It seems that Jonny was using Roger's Special

Olympics pen without asking, and Roger took Jonny's book without asking.

MOM: All right, all right, stop this pushing now. Roger, what happened?

ROGER: He took my pen without asking.

MOM: What were you trying to do by shoving him?

ROGER: Get my pen back.

MOM: What else?

ROGER: Er, um, blurble.

MOM: I can't hear you.

ROGER: Get him back.

MOM: Jonny, what were you trying to do?

JONNY: He's trying to break my book.

MOM: He is? How do you know?

JONNY: He took my book and put it under his homework papers.

MOM: What else could Roger be doing with your book?

JONNY: Huh?

ROGER: She asked what else I could do with the book—like I told you, I needed something to lean on and your book was out. I don't care if you take it back—I'll get another book to lean on.

MOM: Jonny, what were you doing with Roger's pen?

JONNY: When you asked me to write down "meat" so you'd remember to take it out of the freezer, his pen was out and I used it. Then I went to do my puzzle book, I took it, and I just forgot.

MOM: We'll talk about this more later. But I hope you both realize that your brother may not have had the goal you think he did—he may have had a different reason for doing something than you think. And next time, before you start pushing, first think about what you want to have happen and how pushing will help you get there.

ESP/FLASH COMMENTARY

Encourage your teenagers and their younger (and older!) siblings to express their goals. As you do, you will provide them with the awareness they need to be able to decide on their goals—a skill you will want them to have, especially as they become older and more independent.

BEN AND JERRY'S FOR THE TEENAGE HOLE

PART OF SHOWING LOVE IS TO ACCEPT AND ACKNOWLEDGE WHAT YOU HEAR AND EMPHASIZE THE POSITIVE

When your teenagers get into relationship issues, they are likely to feel that the whole world is against them and that no one— least of all their parents—understands. To help our kids handle these difficulties with emotional intelligence and to keep our kids feeling like we are on their side and at least somewhat under-standing of their issues and concerns, we can look at the positive side of what we hear. Much of what our teens share with us is a type of complaint or criticism, and we understand this tendency as part of their developmental process. Nevertheless, we don't want to make matters worse! So, we recommend that you acknowledge what they are saying and try to emphasize the pos-itive, pointing out that the glass is half full rather than half empty. Let's look at the difference:

MOM: Ben, what on earth are you doing?

BEN: I was really bored. I was going to watch TV, but I figured I'd fix the chair. You said it was a pain, so I took the scissors and cut a hole and put in some padding I cut off the rug pad—no one will see it. Now I'm taping it up and coloring it with Magic Marker so it will be the same color as the chair.

(Half-empty) MOM: How could you do such a thing? Weren't you thinking? That chair is ruined. What's wrong with you?

(Half-full) MOM: So all this work is because you were bored and you decided that instead of watching TV, you wanted the chair to be less of a pain for me? I hardly know what to say.

BEN: What do you think, Mom?

MOM (trying to keep from fainting): You know, I'm afraid I can't try it because the marker isn't dry on the tape yet. I'm glad you were trying to make me more comfortable. Let's talk about how else you can try to do it next time.

ESP/FLASH COMMENTARY

Ben's mom, when seeing the glass as half full, understood the kindness Ben showed in passing up television to do something for her. Although his method wasn't the best, Mom let Ben know that she appreciated his goal, which in this case involved helping someone else. Mom gently shifted the focus to looking ahead to next time, and she used emotional intelligence in choosing to wait until she was a little more calm and ready before talking about Ben's methods. The half-empty approach would have produced shame, anger, and an "I'll show her" point of view, partly because it focuses on the unfortunate choice of *what* to do, rather than *how to do it.*

It's a challenge for parents to keep a sense of perspective and humor and look at the shredded furniture and rug pad as well as a set of decision-making and problem-solving skills teens need to have nurtured. You will have to find your own balance between the present and the future. Regardless of the balance, you will raise a more emotionally intelligent teen by following our suggestions to help them become more aware of goals and how to decide among them.

CONVERSATION STARTERS

We have made extensive use of hypothetical stories and story stems in our work. You can, too. A story stem is best described as part of a story. It is often easier, at first, for teens to react to brief hypothetical situations that they are not involved in. They can answer as if they were one of the people in the story. Next, they can gradually describe what they might do in the hypothetical situation, and then eventually respond to these questions: Has anything like this ever happened to you? How did you handle it? What else might you have tried? What would you try if it happened again?

Story stems such as the ones we will describe are best thought of as conversation starters. From our experiences we have found several types of lead-ins to be useful.

There was this rumor: "I heard that a girl in the middle school was being bothered by other kids on the school bus, and it was really upsetting."

Did ya hear? "In the paper, there was a story about how hard it is for some high school students to do well in gym and how it is frustrating and embarrassing for them."

I was wondering: "I was just thinking about how important it can be to be in a marching band. I wonder...if someone in your school wanted to get into the band, how could he or she do it? What if he or she didn't get accepted?"

Other ideas for lead-ins will occur to you, and you will find your teenagers responding best to one format or another. After a while, they also will realize that this is a "code" you use to state your concerns. When you do a story stem, you may get what you consider to be a troubling solution; if so, encourage you child's willingness to be creative, and also try to examine the possible consequences.

WHOM SHOULD YOUR KIDS HANG OUT WITH?

The car sometimes gives us chances to talk about things that are a little harder for adolescents...and their parents...to discuss face-to-face. In the situation below, Dad has just picked Samantha up after a party, and he starts a conversation with her about it.

DAD: It looks as if there were about three different things going on at the same time outside tonight.

SAMANTHA: There were. There's a lot happening these days, and I don't know what to do.

DAD: I don't understand, Samantha. Sounds like there's a problem.

SAMANTHA: There is. Michelle and her friends want to watch videos and be on the Internet all the time. She and her family think that a V-chip is something you dip into V-salsa, so they have no restriction on their Web stuff. Jeff and that group is into sports, soccer, basketball, whatever is in season at school. Rachel and Melanie and Kristin talk about the hottest guys all the time and want to go clubbing whenever they can. [Reality check: Clubbing does not refer to violent acts against persons or property by youths wielding large wooden objects. It refers to going from one "nightclub" to the next in a given evening, usually but not always on a weekend. Many of these clubs serve alcohol and are more and more careful about admitting underaged youth. Other clubs, such as those focusing on swing dancing, don't involve alcohol. Still, there is the issue of where the clubs are and how teens are going to get there. Like many things in the teenage years, the talk exceeds the doing, and much of what is talked about does not come to pass because of logistical reasons. Don't protest too loudly or too soon, or else you might create the motivation for something to happen to prove you wrong.]

DAD: Are these your main choices? Are there any of your friends who are not in one of these groups? What about your friends from the Youth Group?

SAMANTHA: That's true. I don't see them that often, and I sometimes forget about them.

DAD: What kinds of things do you do with them?

SAMANTHA: I usually see them at local meetings or regional events or dances. They like to dance, we have fun watching videos and sometimes shopping, or going bowling. Laser bowling is the best.

DAD: I would need laser vision correction before I thought about bowling again...it's been a while. Anyhow, you have a lot to think about. How can I help?

SAMANTHA: I don't know.

DAD: Remember, transportation is usually an issue, so you need to check with me before you plan anything.

SAMANTHA: Okay.

ESP/FLASH COMMENTARY

Dad has done great work here. He has helped Samantha make positive linkages by reminding her about a positive group she did not mention. He also remembered that Samantha had previously told him about a group of friends that wanted to go on different fast, scary roller-coaster rides, something that Samantha seems to like. But he refrained from adding that to the mix. We call that "editorial privilege." Dad also did not press the issue. If she decides to do something that he is really worried about, then he can deal with it when it happens. Again, logistics often render teenagers' plans impossible, and we see no good reason to jump into unnecessary conflict. Because he withheld disapproval, Dad has allowed himself to be a resource for future conversations on the topic of friends.

One might ask about that first situation, with unsavory Internet sites and videos. This is a tough call. The main issue is whether your teenager really enjoys these activities. Remember, lots of times they will go but feel uncomfortable, especially if their parents' personal values relating to the issue are clear. Things we forbid too fast take on their own curiosity value and magnetism. The same is true with clubbing. If the group is thoughtful and careful about where they go, there is not much of a problem. We can't assume that because there are potential dangers, the worst-case scenario will occur.

Our role as psychologists now allows us to say something to you that we might have less confidence saying if we were only parents. *Just because your teenagers do something once does not commit them to a lifetime of that behavior.* Teens will experiment, and they need to know that they can come to you with their concerns, fears, and conflicts. While we all want to protect our children from all harm, it is not realistic. If your teenager does associate with peer groups you do not like, you have to be careful in how you respond. Ask questions, set curfews and other limits, but don't assume that your child will follow every bad thing his or her peers do. If you have given your teenager a strong base of values, these values will not disappear so easily.

EVERYTHING I KNOW I LEARNED AT THE DINER . . . NOT

The diner is a complex environment created to torture the decision-making skills and patience of family members, as well as of the wait staff. The menu is often the size of a two-family home and contains numerous inserts and options for à la carte ordering, full meals, or, for those with stomachs the size of Florida, both. The entire situation can be complicated by the fact that the kitchen might not have all the vegetables listed or offer the ones you want and that your waitperson may or may not fully know the menu. Many diners also have jukeboxes, which serve as a major distraction to all children present.

Each visit to a diner challenges us with a complex set of decisions that families cope with in different ways. When it gets out of hand for Ellen and Paul and their teenagers, Courtney and Kelcy, it can go like this:

PAUL: I'm in the mood for some breakfast food.
ELLEN: I'd like a salad, maybe the cottage cheese plate.
COURTNEY: Dad, can I get the tomato soup?
PAUL: Sure. Maybe I'll have soup, too.
KELCY: Soup? I thought you said you wanted breakfast? I'm going to get this *bourekia* thing.
PAUL: What's that? The Greek cheese thing?
KELCY: Yes. It's great!

COURTNEY: They also have a tomato surprise. Maybe I'll have that.

ELLEN: Does anyone have some change? I think I'll play some music...how about Counting Crows? Oh, here's Dave Matthews!

WAITRESS: Are you ready to order?

KELCY: Sure. Are you ready, Mom?

ELLEN: Not yet. I just saw the specials.

PAUL: Maybe I'll have a full dinner.

COURTNEY: I'll start with tomato juice.

WAITRESS: I'll be back later.

Is this chaos, or what? In some families, this is fine. For others, it's better to eat in under three hours. Here, Emotionally Intelligent Parenting can be an asset. Note how, below, the parents start with their feelings, move pretty quickly to some goal setting, and then manage it all with good social skills:

PAUL: I'm in the mood for some breakfast food, and I feel like ordering quickly.

ELLEN: It's always a problem deciding what to order here.

PAUL: Yeah. So let's not make a big deal out of it. How about everyone decide what you feel like eating—then we can decide what music to play.

KELCY: I'm all set with my order.

COURTNEY: So am I. Let's pick three songs to play. How about "Goodie Goodie" by King Sol and the Boys? And "Bennie and the Jets"!

PAUL: Kelcy, you pick the other. Courtney, what did you think of the movie last night?

COURTNEY: It was pretty good.

PAUL: Which of those crazy situations they got into did you like the best?

COURTNEY: Well, there were two...

ESP/FLASH COMMENTARY

Naturally, the waitress didn't come over, because she would never have suspected that any family could decide so quickly. Paul modeled for Courtney his own feelings and the problem of taking so long to order—and Ellen put the problem into words quite clearly. Paul also anticipated several other problems (music, specials) and then was able to go on to other topics, like helping Courtney think more carefully about the movie they had seen. Sometimes raising an emotionally intelligent teenager involves modeling how to take a leadership role and move one's "group" along.

JAKE AIN'T GETTIN' THE GIRL

JAKE: Oh, man, I can't believe it. I just cannot believe it.

MOTHER: What happened?

JAKE: My teacher told me I'm not going to be on the cooking team.

MOTHER: Cooking team? What's so unbelievable about that? You have trouble making toast and buttering it.

JAKE: Yeah, but Judy's on the team and I think she's great. Now I've lost her forever! That's it. Poof! I can't believe it.

MOTHER: Sounds gloomy. So, Judy's actually disappeared?

JAKE: Aren't you listening? She is on the team and I'm not!

MOTHER: Forgive me for being an adult, and even a parent, but am I missing something? Does she spend *all* her time with the cooking team? I bet she must practice at home, and she might even need someone to taste her practice creations.

JAKE: Are you…She wouldn't.…I can't.…Hey, you know, there might be other places I can try to see her besides that stupid team.

MOTHER: Great idea!

Jake had lost track of his true goal: to spend more time with Judy. He made his solution—joining the cooking team—into his goal. Mom was able to take his perspective, empathize, use humor, keep her cool, and help Jake stay focused on his real goal. But restoring a goal to its proper position may not be enough.

JAKE: Oh, oh, oh. You won't believe it. You just will not believe it.

MOTHER: What happened?

JAKE: I was trying to spend more time with Judy, right? So when I got turned away by the cooking team, I tried to help her by tasting what she cooked. And I kept getting those terrible stomachaches.

MOTHER: The doctor said he never saw a skinny teenager like you lose so much weight. Good thing he had worked with those overseas flood victims. He knew how to help you.

JAKE: Yeah, I felt bad for the cooking team, too. Anyway, I got transferred to Judy's study hall to spend more time with her and then found out it was a "no talking" kind of study hall. What's the point of that? It was so frustrating being able to see her but not talk to her. So then, I know she's been meeting with her guidance counselor about colleges and stuff, so I sign up, too. The guidance counselor calls me in during lunch, which is the only time I get to talk to Judy, and sets me up for all this vocational testing because when he asks me what I want to study in college or be in life, I tell him I have no idea. The testing is during study hall, so now I don't even get to see her. But wait, I figure that I should have more extracurricular activities because I'm pretending to be interested in colleges like Judy. So I ask her what she's doing so I could join too and she tells me all about her volunteer work in the Women's Center. I see this as a pretty good way to pick up chicks in case things don't work out with Judy, but then she tells me that only girls can volunteer there. What are they, sexist? Man, I just can't win. This school year is a washout, a total washout.

ESP/FLASH COMMENTARY

Teenagers like Jake sometimes feel that their present goal is their *only* goal. Jake has again "lost" Judy, and to him that means gloom and doom for the entire school year. It takes ESP to realize that sometimes the best thing a parent can do in the face of adolescent exaggeration and catastrophizing is to focus on your child's strengths. Often, parents play a vital role in keeping teenagers' emerging identities balanced realistically. If they are going to dwell on the negative, we need to restore the positive. That's why Jake was broadcasting on Channel S. Here is how the conversation might continue:

MOTHER: It does seem frustrating. But, you know, Jake, I was thinking about that other club you joined two weeks ago.

JAKE: You mean the radio broadcast club?

MOTHER: Yes.

JAKE: It's really great. We get copies of the latest records and special tickets and we get to do the broadcasts. Hey, maybe I can dedicate a song to—

MOTHER (interrupting): What else looks good this year?

JAKE: Ah, nothing.

MOTHER: C'mon, just stop and think for a minute about something that you enjoy.

JAKE: Hmm. You know, Mr. Sloane teaches some good stuff in social studies. He's got us in groups...

With some gentle prodding, we can provide an optimistic refocusing of our teens' goals.

GERALDINE'S FRIENDS ARE HAVING SEX

Teenagers are, as you well know, very concerned about what their peers think of their actions. They ask themselves, "What will my friends think of me?" "What will they say?" "What will they do?" These are the questions that go through a teenager's mind and create what is commonly called *peer pressure*. Our task as parents includes helping our children make plans that reflect their own goals. We define peer pressure as pressure to follow other people's goals for you. That's why it's important that families are clear about their values and mission and goals. When tough decisions come along, such as the following example about peers pressuring a girl to have sex, teens need to know where their parents stand and why.

Notice how Geraldine's father helps with a difficult situation:

GERALDINE: It's impossible. They want me to go along and I know what they'll say if I don't.

FATHER: Are you using your crystal ball again? I thought I was the only one who had one.

GERALDINE (sarcastically): Is there a point to that comment? Have you been reading parenting books again? [Dad says nothing here—that is his best intervention, regardless of how angry he might be or how tempted to say something that begins with, "Listen to me, young lady..."] I am talking about something serious, Dad. Michelle and Janet have been doing some things that have been getting them into trouble at school, and they want me to join in. I really can't tell you much more, or you'll get angry.

FATHER: Well, if you don't want to tell me, there's not much I can do about it. I don't think I'll get angry, though. It sounds like you've thought about this a lot. What do you think is the best thing for *you* to do?

GERALDINE: They both have boyfriends and they have started, you know, having sex. They tease me because I haven't. They may not hang out with me anymore if I don't.

FATHER: Maybe not. But what do you think is the *best* choice for *you?*

GERALDINE: Hmm. Well, I don't think I am ready to have sex. They should respect that. They would if they were really my friends.

FATHER: I agree with you. Friends should respect the values of their other close friends.

After his daughter left, the father immediately went to the first-aid kit for some serious smelling salts. Sex is one of the toughest topics for families, especially opposite-gender parent-kid combos! There are things that make sex easier and harder than ever to discuss with teens. First of all, their access to information via the media is tremendous. Many teens have familiarity with things about sex that parents did not know until well into their adult years...if then!

Second, there is so much hype around sexuality that it appears to be quite the norm. As in the vignette we presented, which was based on several clinical cases, it's not uncommon for teens to feel the pressure that "everyone is doing it." But the reality is quite different. Teenagers in groups tend to overstate their sexual activity. When we speak with them individually, we find that much of what they say in groups is either exaggerated or out-and-out lies to save face. Thus, a group impression is created that "everyone is doing it." (This is equally true for drug and alcohol use, by the way.) Those who actually *are* doing something then try to bring in recruits to help dispel·their own doubts, along the lines of "misery loves company."

ESP/FLASH COMMENTARY

As parents, we need to know what the schools are doing about issues of sexuality and relationships and to work with our children accordingly to reinforce or correct, modify, or supplement what teens are hearing. Then we have to be clear about the messages we have been sending regarding such things as sex, smoking, alcohol, and drugs. If we have been strongly and clearly opposed, our kids will know that and will be likely to feel anxious about going against our values (regardless of what they might tell us and certainly regardless of how things look with their peers). In such instances, we need to make the point to our teens that a lot of what goes on is exaggeration, that we can't be sure of the real story, and that to do something as serious and potentially life-changing as having sex or taking drugs out of fear of loss of friendship is to give the friend much too much power.

If we have not been clear on our values, then this is the time to do so. What do we really want our teenager to do and why? Have we been clear? Are we clear now? The parenting survey we took earlier and some of our other activities are designed to help us better see what has shaped and what continues to shape our parenting values. Let your teenager know what you think, using your ESP: What are your feelings, your worries and fears? Try to take your teen's perspective: Is this about sex or friendship? If the latter, then you can often refocus around that as a goal. Remember to speak calmly and tune in to Channel H, or you will lose communication in the future.

Help your teenagers select and set a positive goal and plan how to get there. In this case, their goal is to have friendships that don't ask them to do what they don't want to do or, even if they do want to, they may not feel is worth the risk. Then ask your teenagers what action they intend to take and provide feedback on whether you think the action will lead to their goal. And encourage them to keep talking with you. The tougher the topic, the more important it is for us to not push our teens away with our own worries, fears, or disapproval.

ALTERNATIVES TO RUNNING AWAY FROM EMBARRASSMENT AND TEASING

Let's listen in on two high school–aged brothers talking with their parents about some potentially bad consequences of an accident one of them had with their principal.

GROVER: I am so embarrassed!

ERNIE: What happened?

GROVER: I was serving food in the cafeteria and a bug flew right by me and I got scared and dropped the tray.

MOM: Anything break?

GROVER: Mom, you don't understand. The food landed right on the principal, Dr. Molloy.

ERNIE: Oh, man, really! That's hysterical. And he always wears fancy suits and shirts. What'd you do to him? Did they fire you?

DAD: Ernie, that's enough. What happened next, Grover?

GROVER: Everyone laughed at me. And Dr. Molloy wiped off his face.

ERNIE: His face? Foodface Molloy! All right!

GROVER: He asked me to come to his office. He was really mad. Then he took me back to the kitchen staff and said in front of them that I could keep working but I couldn't serve for a month. Well, I can't go back there tomorrow. They'll laugh at me and I'll feel terrible.

MOM: I can see that. But what else will happen if you don't go back?

GROVER: I'll lose my service credits—and I need those to graduate!

MOM: Maybe we can work on ways to handle the teasing you'll get when you go back...

Some kids laugh things off and others take them more to heart. Grover was sensitive to teasing, and its impact on him led to a "flight" reaction. Ernie makes it sound like he would not have been worried, and might even have been proud, but of course the situation was not actually happening to him.

ESP/FLASH COMMENTARY

Mom's ESP/FLASH was clearly set to F. She helped Grover realize that he couldn't just withdraw—he might lose his service credits. And, as we discussed earlier, under "Linkages," service activities are very important sources of linkage for our teenagers. So, she began to engage him in selecting a positive goal and planning some alternative ways to handle the teasing he would almost certainly get. She opened the face-saving channel by helping Grover realize that "flight" was not without its costs: Avoiding or withdrawing from the problem might be worse than having to cope actively.

HOW TO GET YOUR TEENAGER TO SHARE WITH YOU ABOUT A BAD DAY AT SCHOOL

When your teens get home from school, do they leave bread-crumb clues for you to follow rather than tell you what is going on? Many parents have this experience. Here is an example and one way to turn bread crumbs into fresh rolls:

MOM: Hi, Frank!

FRANK: Hi.

MOM: How was your day at school?

FRANK: Oh, it was fine, I guess. ["I guess" is the first clue here. There also can be nonverbal clues, like sighing or looking at the ground or the ceiling or mumbling.]

MOM: Mmm. What were some of the good parts?

FRANK: Nothing much, really. Gym was okay. Lunch was good—they had pickles and soup. ["Really" is another bread-crumb word often sprinkled around for you to follow up.]

MOM: Great! Sounds like a regular day. [Mom is being smart here—she is not trying to make rolls until she has gathered enough crumbs. It all depends on whether your teenager actually wants to talk about a situation or not. You can more easily turn them off than on, and one way to turn them off is to be too eager to help.]

FRANK: Yeah, sort of. [You are recognizing the crumbs by now, aren't you?]

MOM: Was there any part of school that wasn't so good?

FRANK: No, not really. Well...no, not really.

MOM: It sounds like you're not very sure.

FRANK: No, I'm, uh, well.

MOM: I think you have to decide whether or not you're going to talk about what happened today. You can talk to me or you can talk to someone else or you can not talk at all. I guess it depends on what the problem is.

FRANK: It's, uh, well, I think I'd like to join the army.

MOM (struggling to use her ESP and Keep Calm!): Well! I'd like
to hear what happened today that had something to do with
the army.

FRANK: In assembly there were some officers...

ESP/FLASH COMMENTARY

Frank's mom recognized the signs of a Channel L broadcast but
had no idea of what she was going to get once she tuned in! This
does happen on occasion, and parents will need to remain relatively unflappable if they hope to keep getting broadcasts. Mom's
strategy is pretty clear: She asked some general questions about
his day until he sounded particularly uncertain. Then she commented on his uncertainty without making a judgment or losing
patience. Next she encouraged Frank to figure out what *his* goal
was. Since only Frank had the facts, it was his decision as to what
to do. She simply brought the matter to a *choice*, rather than have
the conversation continue in the unproductive way it had been
going.

Because she kept Channel L open, Frank felt comfortable making his revelation. And because his mother's answer was nonjudg-
mental and calm, he felt comfortable revealing even more. If
Channel L had been closed, it's very hard to say what might have
happened. Clearly, especially with teenagers and all that occurs
in their lives and all that goes on in their minds, keeping channels
of communication open are important ways of showing them our
love and staying connected with them.

HOW TO RESPOND WHEN YOUR TEENAGER
WANTS TO PICK A FIGHT WITH YOU

There are times when teenagers' feelings of frustration, anger,
hopelessness, or even boredom simply get to be too much for
them to contain. They feel they have to vent, and to them you
look like you have a sign hanging around your neck that says,
"Vent here, please." Of course, it all usually happens much more

subtly than this. If you are alert, as Sally's dad is in the example below, you can make the best of the situation:

SALLY: What an ugly tie.

DAD: Really? I've worn it before.

SALLY: It doesn't even match anything.

DAD: (Looks down at his clothing but says nothing.)

SALLY: What's this?

DAD: Eggs, scrambled the way you like them!

SALLY: Are you kidding? Those eggs are runny. I'm gagging just looking at them. You sure don't cook like Mom did.

DAD: Hmm.

SALLY: Did you make your mud coffee again? How can anyone drink that slop...weird.

DAD: Sally, what is it that you want to have happen?

SALLY: What?

DAD: What are you trying to accomplish by talking that way to me?

SALLY: I'm not trying to do anything.

DAD: Do you want me to answer anything you've said?

SALLY: No, I don't care. Well, yes. Well...uh, I don't know.

DAD: You've got school and I have work. But we'd better talk about this tonight. I don't like what's going on. Something must be bothering you.

SALLY: Look, Dad, I gotta go. I'm going to finish getting ready.

Sally was spoiling for an argument. This particular example is drawn from one we see often, when teenagers resent that a parent, in this case the mother, is not in the household anymore. Her dad, who must now feel like a radio engineer, recognized the messages on Channel A. He did not plunge in by responding to Sally's comments or by becoming insulted and showing anger. He knew something about her feelings and point of view, and his own, and he kept his cool and did not say anything he would regret later...though he was tempted!

Instead, he tried to help Sally select a positive goal and then come up with plan of action—to talk later. This strategy broke the cycle of angry comments by Sally because she had to *stop and think*. Notice also that with our hectic lives, we often cannot finish the conversations we start. Rushing through a sensitive issue can backfire. Rather than risk that, he wanted to keep the lines of communication open and shift channels. We also need to trust the process: If Sally really wanted to finish the conversation, she would have said so. She had the chance. Generally, even serious conversations can wait until later the same day or very soon thereafter.

SUPPORT YOUR TEENAGER IN TOUGH TIMES: KEEP THE GLASS HALF FULL

We have spoken about teens' tendencies to exaggerate and see catastrophe on the horizon. They are not totally unaware that they are doing this and will send us signals, often along Channel S, that they want us to refocus them a bit and not address the problem as seriously as they present it.

FATHER: You look a bit down. How was your exam?

RAMÓN: I've never had a test like that. Those questions on figuring out the taxes were unbelievable. I'll probably get a D if I'm lucky.

FATHER: That's disappointing, all right.

RAMÓN: And that's it for the scholarship. A two-year college won't be so bad, I guess. I probably couldn't do the work anyway.

FATHER: I think I'm missing something here. It's a big jump from one test to a two-year college, no? Or maybe you are not the same person who came in last week with some good grades and well-done assignments. Can I get that other kid back?

RAMÓN: How can I get a scholarship if I fail a test? And then how can I go where I want to go?

FATHER: What's your goal for the class? How well would you like to do?

RAMÓN: I'd like to get at least a B.

FATHER: Uh-huh. Is that impossible?

RAMÓN: You know, I bet I still can, depending on how the grading is done.

FATHER: It would not surprise me if the grades were all probably lower than usual. But you have not even gotten it back yet!

RAMÓN: I'm going to check on it tomorrow with Mr. Block.

FATHER: What if Mr. Block says he can't do anything about the grade and it does turn out to be what you think? How can you still reach your goal?

RAMÓN: I'm not sure. But if I talk to Mr. Block about it, maybe there is something I can do to make it up, or get extra credit.

FATHER: What if he still says no?

RAMÓN: Hmm…He wouldn't be such a jerk.

FATHER: Still, there may be policies. What else can you do?

RAMÓN: I could go talk to my guidance counselor. I also might go to the vice principal, who likes me because he knows you and Mom from helping out at the teachers' breakfast all the time…

ESP/FLASH COMMENTARY

In this example, Ramón had a temporary setback. His father was supportive and helped him see the big picture—beyond the single exam to the overall course. With his goal fine-tuned, Ramón was ready to take an active stance and talk to his teacher. His father opened the support channel, and Ramón responded.

HOW TO HELP WITH HIGH SCHOOL HOMEWORK

We don't want to speak for you, but lots of high school kids are doing schoolwork that we don't know how to do. Maybe we knew once—in college, maybe. Perhaps we are of some use in one or two subject areas. But a lot of what they will bring home will be beyond us. How can we be useful sources of help to them?

NICOLE: I've had it! That's it! Forget it!

MOTHER: What's going on?

NICOLE: When will I ever need Spanish? I'm going to see my guidance counselor. Mrs. Rosen will switch me to something else, I know she will.

MOTHER: It seems as if you've been working on the Spanish for a long time.

NICOLE: Over an hour!

MOTHER: What exactly are you doing? I'd like to see.

NICOLE: Don't bother—what a waste.

MOTHER: No, really. I'd like to get a better idea of what they're asking you.

NICOLE: All right. Here, see?

MOTHER: This *does* look hard. How do you try to figure out which tense to use?

NICOLE: I just look at these examples.

MOTHER: Is there anything else I could try? Those examples don't seem too helpful.

NICOLE: Yeah, I guess not. I probably should have tried something else, or—I know! We have a handout that I bet would help. Or maybe I could ask Carlos or Rosa. They seem to know what's up with the tenses.

ESP/FLASH COMMENTARY

Outbursts of frustration are pretty clear signs that help is needed. But parenting with emotional intelligence means that we try to evaluate the feelings before jumping into action. Nicole's mom started by showing she was interested, concerned, and understanding. Notice how she asked how she, the mother, could help. She empathized clearly with Nicole's difficulties, rather than belittling her or minimizing them.

A basic rule when tuning in the help channel is that it's usually not up to us to decide if help is needed. Our teens have already decided that. And it's also not up to us to tell them how helpful all the things in front of them are. If those things were so helpful, our teens wouldn't be in the situation they are in now. So it's a good idea to look to other resources at the moment. Show your love. Be sure the limits are present: You expect her to get the work done, not give up. Make linkages: If you don't know what to do, help her find those who can. If we are hopeful *and* planful, we provide much encouragement to our teens.

LEONORE AND GYMNASTIC STRESS, AND NELSON THE DREAMER AND READER

"No, no, no. More lift—*more lift!*" Leonore's gymnastics coach had never been easy on her, but this was the roughest day she could remember in her fifteen years. As she kept trying the routine on the uneven bars and as she kept hearing her coach's criticisms, she noticed she was having more and more uncomfortable feelings. "The last time I felt this way was when my friends were sleeping over and Dad blew a make-believe trumpet and said it was time for us to go to sleep—and that was only two weeks ago." Leonore thought about this as she put some chalk on her hands. She got ready to try again. As she looked at the bars, she imagined herself doing the routine better than ever. She noticed other, good feelings joining the uncomfortable feelings she'd had before. When Leonore completed her landing, she knew she had done well. She knew she was feeling proud of what she had done. When her coach said, "Not bad—next time, more fluid, more graceful," she felt a warm feeling that she had come to learn meant joy. These feelings stayed with her as she changed in the locker room, before she met her friends.

Her friends Raquel and Alicia asked her how her practice went. Their question started Leonore thinking. "It was an amazing day. My coach kept criticizing me, and I had all kinds of feelings. I felt *angry* because he kept saying I needed more lift. I felt *disappointed* because I wasn't doing the routine correctly. And I even felt *embarrassed* when I thought about what my father did at my sleep-over party—you remember." "We sure do," they said. "At least he can carry a tune." "Yeah," Leonore agreed. "Well, when I stood at the bar, I told myself why I had all those feelings, and I didn't feel so confused and upset. When I thought about doing the routine well, I felt hopeful. And when I finished and the coach said, 'Not bad,' I felt proud because I knew I had done my best routine today." "What a day!" Alicia said. Raquel added, "It's great to hear. I hope you'll show us the routine..."

Leonore enjoyed being with her friends and looked forward to her next practice routine. At age fifteen, Leonore knew she could sort out her feelings, put them into words, and keep things in focus better than a lot of other people her age. She had good ESP skills. As she walked home, there was a bounce in her gait that reflected the smile on her face.

Nelson liked reading about Indiana Jones, Sherlock Holmes, and other adventurers. They kept cool in the face of danger and mystery. They kept their wits about them; they thought fast and clearly. They could tell what a problem was and *zoom*—they started to deal with it. Sure, Nelson was only sixteen, but it seemed hopeless. Those guys were sports cars; he was a station wagon. They were Learjets; he was a transport plane. They were filet mignons; he was an undercooked meat loaf. They were...

"Hey, Nelson, what are you doing? You look fogged out." "No, Lee, I was just thinking about this book I'm reading." "Are you going to Hollie's picnic next Saturday?" "What picnic?" "Oh, ah, um, I don't know. Listen, I gotta go finish looking up stuff for my report. See you later!"

Nelson said good-bye and went back to his reading. Who cares about Hollie's picnic, anyway? But he started having trouble— many upset feelings kept him from enjoying Sherlock. When he switched to Indiana Jones, nothing changed. He kept asking himself, "Why do I feel like this?" He became restless and fidgety. Lee came back to see if Nelson was ready to leave. "Hey, Nelson, let's head out, I'm going to the movies tonight." "When I'm good and ready." "What's the matter?" "Just bug off, Lee." "Hey, Nelson, I mean, hey...what's going on?" "Hollie's not so nice, either." "Hollie? Nelson, I'm going. You need a good night's sleep—or maybe a shrink." Nelson sat there, his face getting redder and redder, his hands gripping his book so tightly that the pages got crimped and damp with sweat.

ESP/FLASH COMMENTARY

Teenagers like Leonore and Nelson have a lot in common. They are developing a sense of who they are and what they can and cannot do well. They want to be involved with friends, and they are experiencing very strong and sometimes conflicting feelings. Leonore has developed a way to handle these feelings and turn their energy into constructive action. Nelson is locked up by his feelings. They are confusing and hard for him to separate, and they cause frustration that spills over onto uninvolved others, like Lee. What does Leonore do differently?

Leonore has learned FIG TESPN. She puts her feelings into words. She tells herself what the problem is that has led to the feelings. She felt angry because the coach kept criticizing. The *criticism* was the problem, *not something about Leonore.* And Leonore has learned what we have taught many, many children. What do you do with a problem? *Evaluate, Select, and Proceed!* So Leonore took the energy of her feelings, told herself what the problem was, and tried to meet the challenge of solving it. Her feelings of pride came because she improved her performance and because the coach acknowledged it. These positive feelings were not signs of problems, but it was still rewarding for Leonore to be able to put these good feelings into words and share them with her friends.

Nelson is a sensitive teenager whose upset feelings have left him hopeless and frustrated. If he were able to tell himself what the problem was, he could perhaps try to solve it. Take a moment and review Nelson's story. What problems could he have identified? He felt worthless and inadequate because he was comparing himself to Indiana and Sherlock. He felt left out and angered when Lee asked him to leave, and especially when Lee said he might need a shrink. *Nelson's upset feelings needed labels;* then he had to *tell himself what problem his feelings were signs of.* If Nelson could say to himself, "I'm angry because I wasn't invited to Hollie's picnic," he could start to think about the situation and *make a decision* about what to do next. An adolescent like Nelson, unfortunately, is likely to have angry outbursts that friends, parents, other relatives, and teachers will not understand—that is, until he is helped to develop the competencies he needs.

In Chapter 9, we will tackle some of the tougher situations that face parents in the teenage years. We call it "The Clinical Corner" because we draw from some of the situations we see in our private practices. But above all, we want to help parents think preventively, because the earlier we address problems, the better our chances of success.

Chapter 9

The Clinical Corner

How to Spot and Handle
Tough Situations

What about body piercing, you say? Kids that won't talk to you at all? Kids whose rooms look like Gothic castles, only raunchier? Kids who sleep all the time? Kids who take drugs? Kids who never come home when you want them to? Kids who talk disrespectfully to you and are violent at home? What about them?

First and foremost: Dig through your records on these kids and see if the warranty has expired yet. In most cases, it has. But in some cases, you might be able to get a trade in, a "preowned" teenager. We know, some of you are hesitant..."better the devil you know."

So, you are stuck with them, for the most part. What are you going to do? Are there some simple tips to create changes? Believe it or not, there are forces operating on your family to keep things just as they are. We think it's important that you understand how this works, and in this "Clinical Corner" we want to share with you some reasons it is so hard for families to change on their own. It's simple, really. We can understand it as the development of a habit or pattern of relating. As human beings, we are attracted to patterns. We are not as driven as moths and plants are when they move toward light, but we are closer than you might think. Moths and other insects often end up burning themselves on the flames they are attracted to. Plants grow toward the light, which is a healthy thing in general, but one of us remembers well a jade plant that grew toward the light and shifted all its weight to one side of the pot and then took a nosedive off its shelf. Some of it was saved, but this was a good example of how a natural tendency that is usually good can also be harmful.

So it is with us and patterns. We get used to things and we stick with them even after they might not still be good for us. Families with teenagers have sometimes gotten into patterns of relationships that most members are not thrilled with and yet find it very hard to change. It's frustrating, too, because everyone seems motivated to change! We know it's hard for *us* to change, but we get annoyed at the other family members when they don't change. Unfortunately, these patterns of relating to one another become kind of set. When they are too set and there is too much distress, making changes usually requires some outside help.

But before we discuss those serious situations, we want to review various family situations so that you can see which seems most like yours. We'll also give you some ideas you can try and some indicators to let you know when you might need extra help.

> Parents who are in the midst of a declared or undeclared war with their children over chores and responsibilities should recognize the fact that this war cannot be won....There is only one way in which we can win: by winning the children over. This task may seem impossible: it is merely difficult, and we have the capacity to accomplish it. —Haim Ginott, *Between Parent and Child*

Truth be told, the A, B, and three C's we have used as the framework for this book have been designed to help parents avoid wars with their teens and also to end the wars that do start as quickly as possible, with the fewest casualties or changes in the balance of power. The combined presence of Love, Laughter, and Limits is harder to maintain in difficult times, but they continue to be necessary for the family. Linkages, as we will discuss, are essential when wars do seem to get out of control or when parents find they are too busy fighting to care as much as they should. We need some guidelines to let us know that this is occurring, however. Appreciation, Belonging, Confidence and Competencies, and Contributions will always be the keys to reaching your teens. Severe troubles occur when these are not present, or when they have been eroded; problems also result when a particular aspect that your teen values above all the others has been threatened or lost.

And this is what parents need to keep in mind. Most severe teen troubles are related to a loss of identity, a loss of direction. When touch points for their lives—whether involving academics, peers, careers, sports, hobbies, or another area of personal excellence—are in danger, with them can go your teenager's sense of self, security, and future. The cognitive tendencies to exaggerate that we spoke of earlier make the problem more difficult to them than it looks to you. Catastrophizing interferes with problem solving. Logic on our part will seem like insensitivity. We need to watch what we do even if motivated out of love, give a certain amount of watchful space to them to see if they can regroup, but also be prepared to move in quickly if necessary. And we will look at the warning signs that such actions may be necessary.

But we never want to lose the context of what is happening, and that is our relationship with our teens. Is there anything more precious to parents than their relationship with their children? Not likely. But sometimes the warmth we experienced when our kids were little gives way to the kind of battleground that Haim Ginott describes. In some cases, it is the result of our children growing up, being capable of thinking and feeling on their own, and not always in agreement with the adults around them. In other cases, unfortunate circumstances—such as illness, loss of loved ones, divorce, job loss, or the impact of violence—have filled children's lives with difficulty, leading them to become pessimistic, bitter, angry, or anxious.

IS THIS RELEVANT TO TEENS WITH SPECIAL-EDUCATION NEEDS?

Many children who have special-education needs can benefit strongly from parenting with emotional intelligence, as well as from parallel instruction in social and emotional learning in school. Whether or not adolescents are labeled as "emotionally disturbed," the problems of their lives, as well as the sometimes unpleasant circumstances they find themselves in in school, evoke strong feelings that make learning and retention of learning difficult.

The ones parents need to worry about most are those who despair about the future, who do not feel able to work to solve their problems because they do not believe that their work will result in progress. Some teens do not see the light at the end of the tunnel, only darkness. Why should they proceed through the tunnel? The principles of Emotionally Intelligent Parenting discussed in this book are designed to light up even the darkest tunnels.

REACH FOR THE UNREACHABLE STAR

Do you remember this song from the Broadway show *Man of La Mancha*? Don Quixote saw good wherever he looked. He kept extending his caring and kindness and empathy to others despite their rejection, ridicule, and even physical assault. This may be more than most of us are willing to do, but perhaps we can draw inspiration from his vision. Every child is a star in some way. We must reach toward their strengths, not what they are doing that is most difficult for us as parents. As parents we must never lose sight of our children's assets and their hidden dreams. These are lifelines for our children, and we must never let go, even if our teen appears to be far out to sea. We can't allow ourselves to dwell only on problems.

PATTERNS YOU CAN TRY TO INTERRUPT

We feel it would be helpful to illustrate the kinds of patterns in families that sometimes get out of hand and need changing. Many of the patterns are part of normal family life from time to time. They become problematic when they occur too often, too intensely, and without a sense of the family being able to stop what they don't like. We have seen these patterns across all kinds of families and problems, and we feel it is more important to focus on these than it would be to try to discuss a variety of specific situations. The underlying issues are what matter.

PATHWAYS TO PARALYSIS: TOO MUCH "P" IS.BAD FOR YOU AND YOUR TEENS

Certain things that we, as parents, will find ourselves doing are signs that our relationships with our teens may be in a state of paralysis. The following "P" words describe things we all do as parents. However, when we find that we are relying on them as our main way of parenting—indeed, our main way of interacting with our teens—then we have to be concerned. Using too much of these suggests that we are in the midst of the kind of war that Ginott referred to earlier. When this happens, parents also need to be especially alert to what we discussed earlier about linkages. Sometimes we are just too closely involved with our kids; we are at the point where it's too hard for us to disengage from the conflict. We need to seek out school personnel, school psychologists, guidance counselors, social workers, private counselors, youth group leaders, or even members of the extended family to help out and give a sense of perspective.

Punishing: "If you don't, I will...", "Do it or else."
  If you find yourself using this very often, especially for many little things instead of high-priority areas, and if you find that it is not working, then it is time to rethink this strategy. Punishment is very powerful and volatile as a parenting "weapon." It can do a lot of harm if not used carefully or if used too often.

Prescribing: "You have to", "You will do XYZ in ABC..."
  If the hallmark with teenagers is establishing a sense of identity, we have to try to give them a certain amount of freedom

within limits. Because they will test us, we have to remember that we can't all of a sudden clamp down on them the first or second time they break the rules. Try flexibility within limits. For example, "You were late last week. I want to know what time you can guarantee me you are going to be home, and it can be no later than one A.M." "You told me there was going to be no alcohol at the party last weekend and there was. What has to happen so that you and I can be sure there will be no alcohol at the party this weekend?" "You told me you had no homework and it turned out that you had two assignments due. How am I going to know that your work will be done before you go to the game?"

Proclaiming: "This is right"; "You must"; "You should..."

This is a variation of prescribing. The big difference here is that many teens resent it when parents seem like the complete arbiter of all that is correct, and do so without explanation or, if asked, resent having to give an explanation. At the very least, teens will respect, and learn more, from hearing your reasons.

Pontificating: "When I was your age..."; "I remember..."; "I once read..."

A certain amount of this is quite healthy, but it depends on how you are doing it. Are you doing it to reflect and share, or are you doing it to suggest that the old ways are still the best ways? If you find yourself spending a lot of time parenting from the past, you certainly need to step back and see how your recollections are going over. You may notice your kids' eyes are glazing over... if they are even in the room listening to you.

Presenting: "What I think you should do is..."; "Here is what's best..."

Again, this is really a matter of style. Of course we present things to our kids, but at some point, especially as they enter their late teens, we need to acknowledge that they might have other ideas about what is "best."

Passing Judgment: "You are not trying"; "You don't care"; "You are lazy."

It's very difficult to look into the souls of our children and correctly ascertain what is in there. Yet as we become more and more sure that our teenagers are "bad"—let's not play around with words here—it will be harder and harder for us to appreciate them, to encourage their belonging, and to see them as contributors. The most parents can feel confident about is describing their teens' actions, as clearly and objectively as possible; be more hesitant about the reasons and motives. There are teens, for example, who care so much about success that they won't try, so as to not risk failure. They are not lazy or indifferent; when we label them in a negative way, we actually drive them toward saying, "What's the difference what I do? Why should I try or care?"

Predicting: "You will fail"; "You will never succeed"; "You will fall asleep"; "The teacher will never let you..."

This is a variation of the above, and we have talked about this issue. Put away your crystal ball. Don't be so sure about what will happen. As we tell students whose parents have convinced them that their future is bleak: Try anyway. Maybe there will be a mistake, a clerical error of some kind, and you and your work will be accepted. But we have a harder time convincing parents. So back off the predictions! As the saying goes, "Be careful of what you wish for, because it might come true."

Probing/Penetrating: "Tell me all the details"; "What did you do? What next? Who else was there..."

Most teenagers don't like to be interrogated. They feel as if they are being put under the hot lights, with the only thing missing an injection of truth serum. But most of all, they feel as if you don't trust them. Maybe you have good reason not to trust them. However, if you pretend that your parent-child relationship is modeled after *Law and Order* or *America's Most Wanted*, you are likely to create only resentment and evasion. Ask a few questions, but then back off. Save further inquiries for later, or perhaps ask yourself if you really need all the details. If you can't keep from probing, there will probably be a serious trust problem between you and your teenager.

Pardoning: "There is nothing to worry about"; "You will feel better"; "Everything will work out despite what happened."

This seems like the opposite of much of what we have discussed, but it is no less important. Teenagers don't want to be parented by the Brady Bunch or Pollyanna. Is there a way of being real without being in denial? Too often, parents want and need to believe that things are going to get better, because they don't know what do to and/or how they can put in the time to do what might be necessary to turn things around. Parents, the sooner you deal with problems, the better off you, your teen, and your whole family will be. When you, in your heart of hearts, know there is a problem, denial should be nothing more than a river in Egypt. Get into action, use your linkages, and find your teen the help he or she needs.

BUILDING BRIDGES TO AND FOR YOUR TROUBLED TEENAGER

What can you do as you try to build a positive bridge with your troubled teenager? It's really a matter of focusing on certain aspects of ESP—Evaluate, Select, and Proceed. Here are our favorite techniques for turning relationships with teens in a more positive direction:

Evaluate

Empathize: Just show that you understand their feelings. Don't analyze.

Ask about your teen's feelings: "How did you feel about that?" "What were you feeling when she said that to you?"

Give your feelings about what you are hearing: "When I hear about accidents like this, I feel anxious, because I worry that you might get involved in something like that and I care about you." Make sure you use this "formula": When I hear about...I feel... because...Teens might not want to hear this, but they will notice that you are really expressing your concern for them.

Reflect: Recall how the current situation relates to a past one that your teenager was able to overcome.

Ask for more information: Ask for descriptions of situations rather than guessing or making judgments. It's fine to say, "Without more details, it's really hard for me to comment, or to know what you mean."

Select

Offer to stop and talk later: Just make yourself available. It's often hard, with our hectic lives, to find time to talk the moment a situation takes place. It is of great value just to let your teens know that you are willing and able to talk when they are ready.

Ask what you can do that would be helpful and about what's next: "How can I be of help to you?" "What is going to happen next? Can I help in any way?"

Proceed

Give constructive criticism: When our relationships with our teens are not the best, things that we think might be helpful can sometimes increase the distance between us and our kids. Before giving criticism, be sure that it does not give you pleasure to do so, that you offer specific ways to change, and that you are able to do so in a reassuring manner. If you follow all three of these guidelines, you can be confident that your criticism is constructive. If not, then you might want to rethink what you were going to say, or perhaps consider not saying anything at all.

RUTS FAMILIES GET INTO AND HOW TO WORK YOUR WAY OUT

When teenagers get into difficulties frequently, their families often wind up in a sort of crisis mode. Patterns start to get hardened and family members, especially our teenagers, get caught in—for lack of a more technical term—a "rut." There is a lack of positive energy in the family. It's like everyone has iron-poor blood and needs an infusion of Geritol. Such situations can be hard to dig out of without some extra help. Members of the family can start to become disconnected and feel like outcasts. The E.I. Transfusion box on this page shows just what we mean.

WHAT MAKES FOR A FAMILY SITUATION WHERE AN EMOTIONAL INTELLIGENCE TRANSFUSION IS NEEDED

Overload: everyone working too hard, not enough fun, not enough family fun

Unfairness: people in the house being treated differently without clear reasons, such as siblings of different ages

Too Little Connection: the family doesn't do much as a family, with relatives, or with family friends; when you do, teens are not involved; neither you nor your teens are linked to schools or to positive peers

Conflicting Values: between parents, between parents and stepparents, between adults and teens

Autonomy Extremes: when family rules for teens are either overcontrolling or not kept track of adequately

Skimpy Rewards: lack of appreciation, both material and personal

Tiredness: members of the household appear chronically to not be well-rested or to be exhausted from household stress, responsibilities

---

There certainly are things you can try before and while you are seeking some extra family help. Here's how to give your family an Emotional Intelligence Transfusion:

• Clear up family goals and how everyone fits in: Cultivate self-monitoring and encourage people to talk about how they are doing with regard to their responsibilities; take the position that it's not easy being a family now and we need to work together, help each other, and give each other ideas.

• Deliver assessments with care: When you are telling a teen how he or she is doing, do it very carefully so as to not hit the "off" switch.

• Teach skills: There is a lot that teens need to learn besides how to drive: how to make a contribution to the family, how to prepare for the tasks of everyday life, how to clean up after company, how to cook a meal, how to clean up after cooking a meal, how to shop efficiently, how to keep track of phone bills and credit card charges, how to set up savings and checking accounts, how to take care of their siblings, how to organize themselves to get their work done. These are all skills, and some kids benefit quite a lot from help with these.

• Provide models: Link your teen with positive role models for character, for skill building, and so on.

• Encourage practice: Skills take time. Be patient, forgiving, instructive, and supportive.

• Arrange support: Encourage your teen to start a local or E-mail support group for teens who have to do dishes or laundry. They can exchange complaints as well as discuss detergents that appear to be the least harmful to their tender teenage skin.

• Encourage and reinforce: Don't expect what you want to have happen just because you want it; find ways to encourage it, ideally with minimal nagging.

• Make change self-directed: As implied earlier, get your teenager involved in self-monitoring; help where help is asked for.

• Give performance feedback: Especially with household

tasks, help your teenagers improve and learn the ever-greater nuances that will truly come in handy when they become adults.

• <u>Expect and prevent relapse:</u> There will be slumps, changes in motivation, even refusals; expect these as part of the natural course of progress and resist the temptation to say something helpful like, "You see, I knew it would never last. It's all back the way it was. You can't follow through with anything..."

• <u>Be patient:</u> Present the positive opportunity and path; know that change is very difficult for everyone and that no one really wants to admit they were wrong. Give teens a way to find their way back, to save face. Resist saying, "I told you so." That is the equivalent of a declaration of war.

• <u>Use humor:</u> Where would we be without this? Keep your sense of humor close by...along with a box of tissues.

SERIOUS RESPONSES TO SERIOUS ISSUES: PARENTS CANNOT WAIT FOR OTHERS TO ACT

Adults should not assume that a young person, simply because he or she knows what is harmful, will act accordingly. Like many of their elders, adolescents often engage in wishful thinking and the hope...that they will personally escape the consequences of what they know to be harmful behavior....It is as perilous for young people to place irrational faith in the corrective power of future adulthood as it is for parents and other adults to shrug helplessly in the face of undesirable or dangerous adolescent behavior, in the expectation that the difficult "phase" will pass on its own accord. —Fred Hechinger, *Fateful Choices: Healthy Youth for the Twenty-first Century*

With this, we introduce our final section, designed to help you act in the face of difficulties being experienced by your teenager. Parents must keep their eyes and ears and hearts open to signs of distress not only in their teenager but in the family as a unit. Richard Jessor, a psychology professor at the University of Colorado and the author of many books on adolescent risk, reminds us that the vast majority of teen misbehavior can be understood as a call for help. They *know* better, but their needs are emotional. It is a cry for A, B, and the three C's. And it typically is a cry that is not just heard in the home; usually, school and peer relationships are touched by adolescent problems. Rebellion or revolution? A phase or a negative trajectory? There are tough calls for parents, so we will try to provide some emotionally intelligent ideas for your use.

MOTIVATION, SELF-CONTROL, AND DELAY OF GRATIFICATION: HARDER THAN YOU THINK

Nearly all parents have spent a sleepless night, a stomach-churning evening, or a frustrated morning asking themselves these questions:

Why is Bobby so unmotivated? All he wants to do is work at the computer and listen to his music.

Why can't Lisa control herself? She doesn't sit in one place for more than a few minutes.

Every time the phone rings, or if she gets a message from her friends, Melanie must go answer it. Why can't she wait and get the things done that she *has* to do before doing these other things?

Raising an emotionally intelligent teenager requires one to be quite empathic and self-reflective. We are not ourselves always highly motivated, self-controlled, or willing to delay what we want. Here are some things you can do that will help you see a little more clearly what your teenager may be feeling and why some of their difficulties are so hard to change.

Step 1: Think of a time recently when you lacked motivation to do something you know you had to do. What was it?

Step 2: Reflect on what it was that made this task hard to do. What things kept you from starting?

Step 3: Now think about a time when you were able to force yourself to get to something you had been avoiding. What got you going? What enabled you to motivate yourself, to tackle something that had been tough for you to get started?

One group of parents with whom we worked gave us answers like the following. About why they had trouble geting started, they said:

- Not fun.
- Didn't know where to start.
- It seemed so long, so large that I was afraid to start it.
- I am a perfectionist and I didn't know the best way to do it.
- I had better things to do.
- It was a boring task.
- I didn't think it was fair that I got stuck doing it.
- I didn't understand what I was supposed to do, exactly.
- I was afraid I didn't know how to do it and was too embarrassed to ask for help.

How did they overcome these difficulties? Groups of parents are consistent in coming up with responses like these:

- I broke up the task into smaller pieces.
- I found others to help me.
- I gave myself rewards for doing each piece.
- Money.
- I talked to others who were feeling the same way, and we started to figure out how we might do the work in a cooperative way.
- They didn't get overcome—I never did it.
- I was afraid of the consequences of *not* doing it.
- I visualized the completed task and how good it would feel to have it accomplished.

What is the point of doing this? Well, when your teenager does not do a task, procrastinates, gets distracted, or can't change a bad habit or other negative behavior, you need to think about yourself in similar circumstances. Very often, things that come our adolescents' way to do are not compelling. This is all too true in the media-driven society many of us find ourselves in. A little more empathy, and a little more help in dealing with the emotions of your teenager with Love and Laughter and Linkage supporting the Limits, will go a long way.

SIGNS YOUR TEENAGER NEEDS HELP OUTSIDE THE FAMILY

Certain kinds of things on our teenagers' minds are indicators that they are likely to benefit from speaking with someone other than their parents. You might get wind of them if you listen and watch carefully for the extent to which they:

* put themselves down and also talk pessimistically about the future and the world in general;
* avoid separation from the family or certain very close peers, with whom they might seem to have an unhealthy attachment;
* display a general sense of worrying, apprehensiveness, and tension, usually accompanied by physical symptoms;
* show specific fears that seem to limit activity and social contacts; these could involve a fear of scrutiny, being the focus of attention, or doing something humiliating;
* repeat compulsive behaviors, rituals that reduce anxiety but seem unusual and evoke an intense reaction if one tries to stop them;
* think obsessively about certain people, events, possibilities, worries, or fears that seem to intrude into a variety of situations and conversations, often inappropriately;
* experience extreme panic attacks, feelings of intense terror, trembling, sweating, breathing difficulty, or other strong physical reactions in response to the possibility of some occurrence, such as being in a crowded place, speaking in front of a group, choosing an outfit, seeing certain friends or family members, or potential dates;

- suffer from stress reactions, in response to a frightening event or occurrence; acute reactions should begin to improve within about four weeks of the event;
  - feel persistent sadness and hopelessness;
  - withdraw from friends and previously enjoyed activities;
  - show increased irritability, agitation;
  - change eating or sleeping patterns;
  - lack concentration, become forgetful;
  - have low energy, motivation;
  - show recurring themes of death, suicide;
  - indicate overall dissatisfaction with life;
  - feel alienated;
  - associate with a negative peer group.

If you suspect something:

- don't minimize your concerns;
- don't think all that is needed is reassurance;
- be patient with your teenager but not with the situation;
- keep the channels open, especially for support and help;
- listen, listen, and listen some more;
- don't hesitate to talk to school personnel, the family physician, members of the clergy, or the police if you suspect that your child might harm himself or herself or others (there will be lots of time later to apologize if you acted in error); a lifetime is often not enough to make up for not acting on what turns out to be a valid concern;
- continue to look for opportunities to provide your teenager with A, B, and the three C's;
- compliment your teenager on his or her strengths.

With these important and serious matters, we want to take a stronger stand: *If you are concerned about your teen, do not ask them if they want to talk to someone; take them to talk to someone.* Never underestimate the power of avoidance. If you think your teen is suffering, it is your responsibility to get help. Do not assume that your child is "grown up enough" to make his or her own decisions regarding this matter. You are the parent, and it is still your responsibility. Of course, your teen may be extremely resistant or hostile, blame you, tell you that it is a waste of money, and so on. Do not be intimidated. Let the professional worry about the teen's resistance. After all, that's the professional's job! If the person is experienced, he or she will not only know how to deal with it but will also be expecting it. Someday, you will be proud to display a bumper sticker that says, "I Dragged My Teen to Therapy." The worst thing that can happen is that the therapist will say your kid doesn't need to be there. Then at least you can stop worrying for a while.

APOLOGIZE WHEN YOU LOSE YOUR COOL

Yes, you will lose your cool at times. Why? Because you are human. You cannot handle unlimited amounts of stress, disappointment, and unmet expectations. Another reason is that our emotional brain systems, which are linked to our identity, lead us to feel badly, or inadequate, when our teens are not turning out as we would like. Rightly or wrongly, these kinds of strong feelings can lead to angry outbursts.

But what does one do afterward? Can hurtful words be erased? In part, the answer is yes.

A parental apology involves a deep understanding of our teenager's feelings, a great deal of self-control, and good social skills, to make the apology "work." What it does for teens is immense. It reassures them about their worth and their value in the world. It lets them know that their parents care enough about them to talk to them in a serious way and admit that they made a mistake. It allows them to learn humility, a companion of empathy. Finally, it alleviates the stress of uncertainty, shame, and doubt that adolescents feel over having provoked—or, in their eyes, deservedly caused—parental over- or underreaction.

Apologizing does not mean that you forget whatever your teen did that was upsetting. Actually, it means that you clarify that some of what you said was hurtful and had to do with your own frustration. But there is a part of the message you want your teenager to get; here are two examples:

- "When you tell me you are going to be in one place and then you go to another, that is unacceptable to me. I feel as if you don't trust me. I know you can keep track of what you tell me and you can remember to tell me where you are."
- "It makes me very unhappy when you hit your brother. It's not a kind or decent thing to do. There are many times when you get along well with your brother, and I know that you can act this way much more often."

The apology follows a formula: I was wrong to say what I did—it was the result of my stress; but here is what I want to make sure you remember and here is the strength I know you can bring with you into situations that might occur in the future.

When it comes time to seek out help, who can provide it? It could be a therapist of some kind, although we urge you to be careful here. Not all therapists are great at working with teenagers and families of teenagers. It is not a part of all training programs. We urge you to look for a specialist who is particularly good with teens, not just families, and to make sure you are convinced that this is the case. You may get references from friends or family members or from trusted sources, such as a pediatrician or family doctor. Many people involved in what are referred to these days as "faith-based" organizations will find them to be a source of help. (For the record, we are not referring here to lottery shops, racetracks, or gambling casinos. We are thinking of more religiously linked faith-based organizations.)

And we also suggest that you think of the school as an important resource. Schools are filled with caring professionals who specialize in working with teenagers. Your school psychologist, guidance counselor, school social worker, school drug and alcohol counselor, health teachers, principal and vice principal, and a number of teachers that your teenagers will be able to identify for you are sources of caring assistance. Sometimes their informal help can make a large difference; in other cases, they can steer you to those who might be able to work with you. At the end of the book, we will talk to you about Emotionally Intelligent Parenting Circles or Networks. We find that this form of parenting support can also be quite helpful when we are not sure where to turn.

Your teenagers may seem to be engaged in serious misbehaviors. But as long as your relationship with them is strong, you keep focused on their good points and not just their problems, and you are using the principles of Emotionally Intelligent Parenting effectively, you will find that they are within your reach. It is important to act, and not to overreact. And it is important to think preventively, which is the main message of this book. By so doing, we fulfill the recommendation of the ancient sages as we "go from strength to strength."

Chapter 10

Something for Teenagers to Read, Especially with Their Parents

Being a teenager is like being a space capsule in an asteroid field. If there are too many asteroids coming at you, especially if they are big and they start hitting you, you forget where you are heading and you just worry about trying to avoid getting hit, and then finding safety. If you do that long enough, you forget where you were trying to go, or maybe you start going someplace else, or maybe you just react to the asteroids and don't really have a destination. A lot depends on your capsule and how strong it is and fast it is and how well it can maneuver.

This is what one teenager said when we asked him to tell his parents what it's like to be a teenager. He also indicated that he thought of the capsule sometimes as himself or his outer shell, and other times he saw his family as the capsule. We didn't pick this quote because it was unusual—just the opposite. The main difference seems to be the size of the asteroids different teens felt were hitting them.

What do you think of this point of view? How would you describe being a teenager? How well do you think your parents understand what it means to be a teenager today?

These are not rhetorical questions. They are extremely important for both you and your parents.

Parents, how do you see your teens' lives? Often, parents view their teens in terms of their own lives. This is not always helpful, because everyone has to be viewed as separate and unique. In addition, the circumstances when your parents grew up and those of today are very different.

This chapter is designed mainly for teenagers, but we want and expect parents to read it also, ideally together with their children. We want to focus on the emotions of being a teenager, of being in a family with teenagers, and of being the parent of a teenager. We are going to do this by asking you—both parents and teens— to do a few things as you read.

IT'S THE TWENTY-FIRST CENTURY: TEENS, DO YOU KNOW WHERE YOUR PARENTS ARE?

Have you figured out your parents yet? Adults are not all that hard to understand. You just have to remember a few basic rules that guide 90 percent of what they do:

1. It was good enough for me, it should be good enough for you.
2. You have to be safe.
3. I want you to grow up, but on my terms.
4. You can have any career you want, as long as it's one that I want for you.
5. Did I tell you about the things I regretted not doing when I was a teenager? How about you do them for me?
6. Your grades are not that important. Neither is oxygen.
7. Did I tell you about the things I did as a teenager? Don't you dare try them.
8. Being clean, neat, and organized is not important to parents, especially not to moms. Water is not important to oceans, either.
9. I can't show you my real feelings, especially not my positive feelings.
10. I can't do enough for you because when I was a kid, my parents didn't do enough for me.
11. I'd like to get a life, but I'm too worried about yours.

12. I really do love you, but it can get lost in all the distractions of life, my own emotions, and the natural conflicts that arise between us.

You might want to rate each of these statements on a 3-point scale, with regard to how true you think they are for your parents. (Parents, if you are reading this chapter, you might want to think about how true each statement is for you.) Actually, for you and your parents to compare notes on this could lead to a very interesting discussion—or argument. But it would be more interesting than a lot of the usual conversations. Here is the scale:

> 1 = Not really true for parents
> 2 = Sort of true for parents
> 3 = Definitely true for parents

Always give the higher score if there is a difference between parents. A score of over 18 indicates that there are at least a few issues where parents and teens need to be clear about who is living whose life and why.

Let's take a quick look at each of these areas:

1. **It was good enough for me, it should be good enough for you.**

Parents sometimes are too deeply rooted in their own experiences. They are not you, and these times are not their times. Parents should ideally reflect this way: It was good enough for me. I wonder how this would be for my child now?

2. **You have to be safe.**

This is motivated by your parents' concern for you, not their need to set limits on you. They did not come this far just to lose you to drugs, AIDS, violence, or car crashes. There is a lot of scary stuff out there. Please be understanding of your parents and responsible with yourselves. We will all sleep easier at night, but not until you come home. There are a lot of things that, if your parents knew would turn out well, they would let you do. But they don't know, and parents vary in how much risk they can stand. It's important that you respect this, but also try to take more and more steps toward greater responsibility. Be patient with your parents when they are motivated out of love!

3. **I want you to grow up, but on my terms.**

Oy. This is a tough one. Some parents have very strong ideas about how teenagers—actually, children of any age—should grow up. This often sets up rebellion, even attempts by kids to avoid the truth or actively deceive their parents. We don't know any honest parents who did not break some rules when they were teens. It's just hard for you to believe that your parents are so all-knowing that they will be correct about everything. For parents, the questions they must ask themselves are, How sure are you that your way is the absolute best or right way? And why are you so sure? We advise parents to have some areas that they feel very, very strongly about but not to be that way about everything. One reason for this is that we, as psychologists, have seen too many families hurt, or even destroyed, by trying to live out one vision of the future. We are not big advocates of using a crystal ball to foresee the future. We believe that parents, and families, need to have values but also need to think about how those values should be put into action in the world as it faces our teenagers today.

4. **You can have any career you want, as long as it's one that I want for you.**

We actually like this rule. Do you know why? It gives us lots of business as psychologists. It drives teenagers, and eventually families, crazy. Not everyone is meant to follow in the family vocational footsteps. We have seen examples of million-dollar businesses destroyed, and family relationships along with them, when children inherited businesses for which they were ill-suited. Smarter by far would have been the selling of the business to those who could and wanted to keep it going, especially if it could continue to generate revenue for the family in the future. We estimate that 10 percent of the time, following a narrow career path outlined by one's parents works out. Teens and parents should be oriented toward finding out if their family is in the 10 percent or the 90 percent, and should not assume anything.

5. **Did I tell you about the things I regretted not doing when I was a teenager? How about you do them for me?**

Parents sometimes try to get a second chance at doing things through their teenagers. One of us remembers doing this with his daughter, having her play soccer. She did not like soccer; at one point, she had to be paid twenty-five cents every time she was hit by the ball—forget about actually running over to it and kicking it. What's up with that? The dad in question had missed his opportunity to be part of organized sports; getting his daughter involved was a kind of second chance. This became pretty clear after a while, and it served as the first of many such lessons. Parents, watch out for this. And teenagers, you have to be willing to sit down and tell your parents that some things are just not for you. Maybe they were fine when you were younger, but they're not anymore. You need to devote your time to things that are of importance or interest to you now. It's not fun to disappoint your parents. But they are adults and they can take it. (If you break the news gently!)

6. **Your grades are not that important. Neither is oxygen.**

This is a tough one. We suggest that you get your parents a present on Father's Day or Mother's Day or both. It's Daniel Goleman's book *Working with Emotional Intelligence*. (We assume you got them our previous book, *Emotionally Intelligent Parenting*, last year. If not, you can get a nice set, with both books!) In that book, your parents will learn that your future professional success will be due 20 percent to your I.Q.—your academic achievement— and 80 percent to your E.Q.—your emotional intelligence, which, of course, is why we have written this book. Your parents can also check out the Web site, www.CASEL.org, which is the home page of the Collaborative to Advance Social and Emotional Learning. There, your parents will learn that the best and most successful schools address both the heads and the hearts of students. They will learn that there must be a balance of grades and constructive social involvement. That's really what we have tried to show them in earlier chapters of the book. Sadly, our society puts too much emphasis on grades and test scores. We want you to be smart, but balance is essential. It takes a lot of courage for parents...and educators...to follow a balanced path. Deep down, they know that it really is the best way. But they worry about the future.

7. Did I tell you about the things I did as a teenager? Don't you dare try them.

This is sort of the opposite of what we talked about earlier. Here, we are talking about parents who had a wild and crazy time as teens and, when they look back on it, wonder how they survived into adulthood. Does that describe a parent of yours? If you are not sure, ask. Many parents don't easily share stories about their youthful adventures. Anyhow, sometimes their cautions are pretty wise, but other times their own experiences can lead them to be overly restrictive. Remember, this is another example of love, not of limits. Parents, you need to reflect on your past and make sure that you are not being excessively cautious. Just because you handled situations in certain ways does not mean that your kids will!

8. Being clean, neat, and organized is not important to parents, especially not to moms. Water is not important to oceans, either.

Face it: Some parents are neat freaks. We are not sexist, but we also know that in the many families we have dealt with, this is more a mom issue than a dad issue. And some teenagers we know love order and neatness more than their parents. Great! But for those teens trapped in a situation where they would prefer creative organization and their parents want traditional organization, we have simple advice: Move. No, not really. See if you can negotiate with your parents. See if there are several aspects of order that they feel are most important that you will do without much hassle (you have to give them some hassle, just to keep them on their toes), as long as they will not hassle you in other areas. For example, you might agree to hang up or put in drawers your newly laundered clothing in exchange for being able to leave lots of nongarment, nonfood, or garbage items on your floor. Or maybe you will pull the blankets over your bed but not have to make it, in exchange for taking care of the garbage or dishes without a reminder (or without many reminders). Parents, don't try to make every battle into a war. Be selective, go for small victories, and keep the peace of your house overall as the most important goal.

9. **I can't show you my real feelings, especially not my positive feelings.**

Some parents, believe it or not, have been brought up to believe that you should not give kids too much praise—or any praise—and certainly not if they do what is expected of them. One of us had a mother who told him that he would get a swelled head. He can remember, as a twelve-year-old, getting praise from a teacher and, especially, from his grandmother and looking in the mirror every morning for signs of cranial expansion. No swelling ever was observed. But lots of hurt took place when good things he did were treated as expected: Of course you did that well. And why didn't you do the rest of it as well? Parents, we have mentioned this earlier, but let's go on record, with your kids as witnesses, as saying that you should show your teenagers your positive feelings toward them whenever you feel them. Let them know how proud you are of them. Let them know that you notice the small things they do. When they bring home an 80 on a hard test, look at that test and see how well *you* would do. That might make it easier for you to start off with praising them for knowing 80 percent (or 70 percent, or even 60!) and later discussing if there is a way you can support them if they feel they should have, could have, or need to do better. And, at the risk of making this too long a paragraph, we add the following note to teens: When you are positive with your parents, they will be more positive with you. Don't take them for granted, either. They often feel as unappreciated as you do. Just because they are parents and should do certain things does not eliminate their human need to feel appreciated and acknowledged and their human tendency to return kindnesses felt with kindnesses given out. Praise can be contagious—start an epidemic in your house!

10. **I can't do enough for you because when I was a kid, my parents didn't do enough for me.**

Another oy. Maybe a double: Oy, oy. It's hard for parents to give what they might not have received. Some parents believe that teenagers need to tough it out. Sometimes, this is a good thing. For example, some parents will pay for certain things but not others. Transportation comes to mind. So does food. Parents of some high school students feel that they can bring lunch from home, but if they want to buy, which is much more expensive, especially if you add it up over 180 school days, they have to pay themselves. Some of your friends might be getting a car, and you are getting carfare. These are issues of upbringing and economics. Parents, we urge you to do one thing: Don't just say "Because I said so," or some such platitude. Explain to your teens why you think it's better for you to give them certain things or do certain things for them, and not others. Sometimes, when we have to make these explanations, it leads to a little useful rethinking. The clearer we are about our parenting decisions, the easier it is to stick to them. Your teenagers might not be happy, but at some level they will at least know that you have given real consideration to your decision. And that might (we said "might," for the legal record!) lead them to nag you less.

11. **I'd like to get a life, but I'm too worried about yours.**

Believe or not, parents do not want to be obsessed by their children's lives. Adolescence is like the homestretch for parents, the last lap. Everyone has made it this far; some are a little behind, some ahead, but everyone can see the finish line: adulthood. (Parents know, of course, and children find out, that this is not the finish line. Parenting and childhood are life marathons.) Some parents may have to work a little harder to make up for missed opportunities; others may want to maintain their lead, and they are not going to take a pit stop now. You may envy some of your friends whose parents have dropped out or given up, but your parents, fortunately or unfortunately, are still working hard at parenting (we know this because they bought this book and have asked you to read this chapter). So bear with your parents.

You are not going to persuade them to get a life other than yours right now. Yes, they need to have balance in their lives, give you some space, and work together with you rather than just telling you what to do, but they are going to maintain their involvement. Sorry.

12. **I really do love you, but it can get lost in all the distractions of life, my own emotions, and the natural conflicts that arise between us.**

We hope that your parents tell you and show you that they love you. This is kind of corny but important for everyone to remember. Life has a way of distracting us from our true feelings and what is most meaningful, which, if you had to pick only one thing, would be love. This is actually more important than grades, friends, cars, and CDs. It is even more important than food, shelter, and clothing, because without love, you would literally have not survived childhood. It is interesting that even though love is so central to people's lives and relationships, it is rarely discussed, especially between parents and teens. So we are encouraging everyone to be aware of LOVE and to talk about it, no matter how weird or awkward this might feel. Yeah, it's like some really dumb, sappy TV movie, but try anyway. Listen, we could have subtitled this book *Limits, Limits, and Limits.* It would have been a bigger seller, and you would be grounded for months. But love and laughter are more fun, and they work just as well, if not better.

STRONG EMOTIONS SEND STRONG MESSAGES: DO YOU KNOW WHAT THEY ARE?

All of the issues we just raised are emotional issues. And so we need to take a moment or two for a look at how emotions are dealt with in your family. First, let's start with everybody's theory about emotions.

In any family with teenagers, emotions are likely to be stronger than when there were no teens in the house. Duh! (Did you ever wonder when you would see that word used appropriately and grammatically in an actual book? Your wait is over!) And teenagers are certainly experiencing stronger feelings than they can remember having when they were younger. But feelings are also messages, and a lot of times clashes between parents and teens are because one is misreading what another is feeling. Sometimes, we just don't realize how strong someone else's feelings are.

Let's start off by sorting out who feels how and what they think should be done with those feelings. Take a look at the Theories of Emotions box on this page. Teenagers, rate which theory (or theories) best describes your views, and also rate what you think is true for everyone else in the house. Parents, do the same things for yourself, your teenager(s), and everyone else in the house. If your teenager spends time at another parent's house, you can decide how far to extend your formal ratings, but you do have something to think about. When you are finished, compare ideas. Also, see if there seems to be an overall family approach.

THEORIES OF EMOTIONS

The Volcano Theory: If you don't vent your emotions, you'll explode.

The Tidal Wave Theory: Don't lose control or your feelings will build up until they overwhelm you.

The Out of Sight, Out of Mind Theory: If you don't think about your feelings, then they will go away.

The Vulcan Theory (from Star Trek*):* Your emotions are irrational and illogical; surely they get in the way of solving problems.

The Pearl Vision Theory: Your emotions are something that need to be looked at as clearly as possible, with as little nearsightedness, farsightedness, astigmatism, or dirty lenses in the way as possible, and then talked about. Sometimes you will act on them, but not always. This will do you more harm than good.

It's not that there are right or wrong answers here, but sparks fly when family members have radically different answers and don't discuss them. Note that we often don't know exactly how or why we have come to adopt the theory or theories we have. Usually it has something to do with our upbringing. We urge you to each try for a little more of the Pearl Vision Theory, as it gives you a bit of useful flexibility. The others have their moments of truth, but teens and parents will run into trouble trying to apply any of them consistently.

Every feeling says something about us and about something outside us, whatever it was that led to the feeling. Look at the following example:

Fright: I am facing immediate, concrete, and overwhelming physical danger.

That's what makes fright so...frightful! There is a sense of danger! That's why some people can go on thrill rides, huge roller coasters that turn you upside down and inside out, or drop you eight thousand feet in the blink of an eye, and others can't imagine going. Those who go do not believe they are in any real danger; the rest of us, most often called *parents* (or, as our kids say, *cowards*), feel fright. There is no good reason to do anything that one feels is truly frightening. The same is true for such things as driving under the influence of alcohol or marijuana. Some teens are not focused on the danger of doing this, while others, and most parents, would be too frightened about likely or possible physical consequences to do it. Of course, alcohol and drugs impair judgment, so once one starts drinking, it is unfortunately possible that the situation will look different. But that's the impact of the drug, not of any change in the reality of the danger.

This is one small example of how helpful it is to understand the messages behind the feelings that people have. Emotionally intelligent family life certainly is helped if we are clearer about what is really going on with our loved ones.

. . .

Let's take the EMQ Test—the Emotional Message Quotient test. We are going to give it to you in two forms, and then we will give you the answers. DON'T LOOK AHEAD!!! In the first form, see if you can provide the message that goes along with the feeling. What does the feeling really mean? The second form is a matching test—we give you a bunch of feelings and a bunch of messages, and you have to match them up. After that, we'll give you the answers. Remember, these are not absolutes. There are different ways to state the messages, and we may have left out some feelings that your family experiences regularly.

1. Anger:
2. Rage:
3. Anxiety:
4. Fright:
5. Guilt:
6. Shame:
7. Deceived:
8. Sadness:
9. Depression:
10. Envy:
11. Jealousy:
12. Disgust:
13. Happiness:
14. Pride:
15. Relief:
16. Boredom:
17. Hope:
18. Love:
19. Compassion:
20. Empathy:

In the following test, try matching the numbers of the correct feelings with their correct definitions. We will provide the answer key, but try it yourself first!

1. Anger

A. I failed to be the kind of person I want to be; I did something or had something done to me that makes me into much less of a person or a worse person than I thought I could ever be.

2. Rage

B. I can feel the way another person feels in a situation; I am experiencing it as that person experiences it.

3. Anxiety

C. I am in a relationship—which may or may not be reciprocated—in which I desire being or am the focus of that person's affection and caring.

4. Fright

D. I am facing uncertainty, something I see as a threat to my status, my comfort, and my physical well-being.

5. Guilt

E. I was involved with or close to an object, idea, or situation that is absolutely foreign to my sense of who I am and what it is that decent people do that is acceptable.

6. Shame

F. I want very badly what someone else has.

7. Deceived

G. I, or something or someone I value greatly, has been put down, diminished, demeaned, or insulted.

8. Sadness

H. I feel that a distressing condition or situation has changed for the better or gone away.

9. Depression

    I. I feel foolish and betrayed because someone I trusted told me a lie and I believed it, making me doubt myself and also whether that person really cares for me and can be trusted by me.

10. Envy

    J. I am moved by the suffering of one or more persons, to the point where I want to help.

11. Jealousy

    K. I am facing immediate, concrete, and overwhelming physical danger.

12. Disgust

    L. I look to the future and think that better things will take place, even if it does not objectively look as if this is the case.

13. Happiness

    M. I have lost or might lose the affection of someone I care about to another person.

14. Pride

    N. I am experiencing an irrevocable, lasting loss.

15. Relief

    O. I feel threatened and offended, to the point where I want to inflict harm on those whom I perceive as causing it.

16. Boredom

    P. I broke an important rule or did not live up to an important value, especially one held by others whom I respect or care about greatly.

17. Hope

    Q. I have a warm feeling about myself, those around me, and what it is that I am working toward accomplishing.

18. Love

R. I have little or no interest in the task or situation in which I am involved, and so I am looking for some kind of distraction or exit.

19. Compassion

S. I have a pretty constant sense of heaviness, joylessness, and hopelessness about the present and future.

20. Empathy

T. I feel like a better and valued person because I was involved in an achievement, either mine or that of someone or a group with whom I strongly identify.

Here is the answer key:

1. Anger

G. I, or something or someone I value greatly, has been put down, diminished, demeaned, or insulted.

2. Rage

O. I feel threatened and offended, to the point where I want to inflict harm on those whom I perceive as causing it.

3. Anxiety

D. I am facing uncertainty, something I see as a threat to my status, my comfort, and my physical well-being.

4. Fright

K. I am facing immediate, concrete, and overwhelming physical danger.

5. Guilt

P. I broke an important rule or did not live up to an important value, especially one held by others whom I respect or care about greatly.

6. Shame

A. I failed to be the kind of person I want to be; I did something or had something done to me that makes me into much less of a person or a worse person than I thought I ever could be.

7. Deceived

I. I feel foolish and betrayed because someone I trusted told me a lie and I believed it, making me doubt myself and also whether that person really cares for me and can be trusted by me.

8. Sadness

N. I am experiencing an irrevocable, lasting loss.

9. Depression

S. I have a pretty constant sense of heaviness, joylessness, and hopelessness about the present and future.

10. Envy

F. I want very badly what someone else has.

11. Jealousy

M. I have lost or might lose the affection of someone I care about to another person.

12. Disgust

E. I was involved with or close to an object, idea, or situation that is absolutely foreign to my sense of who I am and what it is that decent people do that is acceptable.

13. Happiness

Q. I have a warm feeling about myself, those around me, and what it is that I am working toward accomplishing.

14. Pride   T. I feel like a better and valued person because I was involved in an achievement, either mine or that of someone or a group with whom I strongly identify.

15. Relief   H. I feel that a distressing condition or situation has changed for the better or gone away.

16. Boredom   R. I have little or no interest in the task or situation in which I am involved, and so I am looking for some kind of distraction or exit.

17. Hope   L. I look to the future and think that better things will take place, even if it does not objectively look as if this is the case.

18. Love   C. I am in a relationship—which may or may not be reciprocated—in which I desire being or am the focus of that person's affection and caring.

19. Compassion   J. I am moved by the suffering of one or more persons, to the point where I want to help.

20. Empathy   B. I can feel the way another person feels in a situation; I am experiencing it as that person experiences it.

You might disagree with some of these definitions, and of course they are not precise. But we want you and your parents to recognize why you feel as strongly as you do about certain things. In short, the feelings have meaning, and this meaning is sometimes lost to other members of our family. Anger is not just anger; it implies a threat to identity as one is put down, demeaned, or belittled. Anxiety is also about a threat of loss, not just aimless worrying for no good reason. The greater the extent to which family members can state their feelings and concerns and clarify them for one another, the more likely it is that everyone will treat one another's feelings with greater respect and understanding.

PARENTAL EMOTIONS: DO YOU WONDER WHY YOU FEEL THE WAY YOU DO?

We want to add a short section here for the poor parents who may well find themselves having a number of feelings, many of which are outlined above, but still do not know exactly what caused them. Never fear! We have surveyed parents and we have come up with the List of Causes of Parental Attitudes, Perceptions, and Affects (LocoPapa). As you have already seen, parenting a teenager is a great way to build up your emotional range. You are likely to find yourself feeling things you never imagined you would when you were bouncing that kid on your knee. Here are some frequent causes. Teenagers, see if you think that some of these may be operating in your house. Don't expect your parents to admit to any of this.

Bewilderment: You have just received ten minutes of explanation of recent phone conversations your teenagers have had about all that is going on with their friends.

Puzzlement: You were just part of a conversation that ended with, "Thanks, Dad (or Mom)," but you have no idea why or what should have led up to that statement. You instinctively reach simultaneously for your wallet and your car keys.

Disbelief: Your teenagers have told you that they have forgotten something that you have reminded them about many, many times.

Rage: Your teenagers overtly endangered themselves directly or indirectly, including actions that led to a public threat to their (or your) reputation or identity.

Embarrassment: They wear an unbelievable outfit in public.

Mortification: Body art, words and/or graphics, that are visible to friends, family, and/or educators.

Relief: They called to tell you they arrived, even if it is not where they said they would be. Followed soon with worry about their safe return.

Shame: You lied to your teenagers, not for their own benefit but for yours. Or: you got caught in negative modeling.

Fondness: Your teenager did something caring for you, even if accidental.

Pride: Something happened that led you to feel good and think, "That's *my* kid!"

Joy: You see them constructively happy.

Guilt: You made a decision based on your upbringing, not your teens' situation.

Warmth: Results from a positive family meal or outing.

Anger: They defy your authority...or what's left of it.

Envy: Wishing you could do, or ever did do, something they're doing.

TRANSLATION GUIDE FOR TEENS:
WHAT PARENTS SAY, WHAT PARENTS MEAN

We have some translation information for you! You have already figured out that parents sometimes do not say what they mean, and that when you act based on what they said, they seem to get annoyed. How unfair is that? Well, we are here to provide you with a handy guide so that you can avoid some conflicts in the house:

> When your parents say *I'm not worried* ... they are worried.
> When they say *I am worried* ... they are beside themselves.
> When they say *I am a little worried, I have some concerns* ... they are not too worried.

> When your parents say *Do it any way you like* ... it means that they have in mind a way they want you to do it but they don't want to offend you by telling you. You can ask them, though, if you like.
> When they say *I don't think you should do it that way* ... it means that they are anticipating great calamity.
> When they say *That's a good idea, try that* ... it means they are mildly fearful but can handle their anxiety.

Let's try this in another format, something many of you are familiar with from school:

When your parents say *Do it any way you like,* you should:
a) do it any way you like
b) suspect a trap and not do it at all
c) realize that they want you to suspect a trap and this is their way of getting you to not do it at all, which means you should do it
d) try to figure out the way they really have in mind for how they would like you to do it
e) all, none, or some combination of the above

When they say *I am worried,* you should:
a) reach for the cardiac medication and call 911
b) pray for forgiveness
c) call a friend and maybe forget about doing whatever you were thinking about
d) torture them for a while and then do (c), above
e) talk to them about what they think might happen

You don't really need the answer key, do you?

SOME FINAL SUGGESTIONS FOR PARENTS AND TEENS

As you know, the title of this book is *Raising Emotionally Intelligent Teenagers: Parenting with Love, Laughter, and Limits.* It's about the importance of making households less stressful, more understanding, more supportive, and more fun. We want to close with something from Patty Wooten's Web site, http://www.JestHealth.com. Patty and her colleagues are wonderful sources of joy and inspiration for everyday living. You and your parents can use the following list, reading one item per day for a month, and try to live by some of the ideas she has gathered from various sources. Perhaps put the list on your refrigerator. When you are finished, start again. Here are thirty-one ideas, to hold you over through the longer months.

Life Instructions
1. Give people more than they expect and do it cheerfully.
2. Memorize your favorite poem.
3. Don't believe all you hear, spend all you have, or sleep all you want.
4. When you say "I love you," mean it.
5. When you say "I'm sorry," look the person in the eye.
6. Never laugh at anyone's dreams.
7. Love deeply and passionately. You might get hurt feelings, but it's the only way to live life completely.

8. In disagreements, fight fairly. No name-calling.

9. Don't judge people by their relatives.

10. When someone asks you a question you don't want to answer, smile and ask, "Why do you want to know?"

11. Remember that great love and great achievements involve great risk.

12. Say "Bless you" when you hear someone sneeze.

13. When you lose, learn something from it.

14. Remember the three R's:
    > Respect for self;
    >> Respect for others;
    >>> Responsibility for your actions.

15. Don't let a little dispute injure a great friendship.

16. When you realize that you've made a mistake, take immediate steps to correct it.

17. Spend some time alone.

18. Open your arms to change, but don't let go of your values.

19. Remember that silence is sometimes the best answer. If you don't know what to say or do, do no harm.

20. Read more books and watch less TV.

21. Live a good, honorable life. Then, when you get older and think back, you'll get to enjoy it a second time.

22. A loving atmosphere in your home is so important. Do all you can to create a tranquil and harmonious home.

23. In disagreements with loved ones, deal with the current situation. Don't bring up the past.

24. Share your knowledge and talents. It's a way to achieve immortality.

25. Be gentle with the earth, especially the parts you live on.

26. Mind your own business. Certainly don't snoop or eavesdrop.

27. Once a year, go someplace you've never been before.

28. If you make a lot of money or get a lot of gifts, put some of it to use helping others. That is money's greatest satisfaction.

29. Remember that not getting what you want is sometimes a stroke of luck.

30. Your character is your destiny. You can always improve your character.
31. Approach love and cooking with reckless abandon.

Remember, when all else fails...there is always chocolate!

Recommended Readings

Benson, P. L., *All Kids Are Our Kids: What Communities Must Do to Raise Caring and Responsible Children and Adolescents* (San Francisco: Jossey-Bass Publishers, 1997).

Berman, S., *Children's Social Consciousness and the Development of Social Responsibility* (New York: SUNY Series: Democracy and Education, 1997).

Brendtro, L., Brokenleg, M., and Van Bockern, S., *Reclaiming Youth at Risk: Our Hope for the Future* (Bloomington, Ind.: National Educational Service, 1990).

Charney, R. S., *Habits of Goodness: Case Studies in the Social Curriculum* (Greenfield, Mass.: Northeast Foundation for Children, 1997).

Chopra, Gautama, *Child of the Dawn: A Magical Journey of Awakening* (New York: Amber-Allen Publishing, 1998).

Cohen, J., ed., *Educating Minds and Hearts: Social Emotional Learning and the Passage into Adolescence* (New York: Teacher's College Press, Alexandria, VA: ASCD, co-publisher 1999).

Denham, Susanne A., *Emotional Development in Young Children* (New York: The Guilford Press, 1998).

Dryfoos, J. G., *Safe Passage: Making It Through Adolescence in a Risky Society* (New York: Oxford Press, 1998).

Elias, M. J., Tobias, S. E., and Friedlander, B. S., *Emotionally Intelligent Parenting: How to Raise a Self-Disciplined, Responsible, Socially Skilled Child* (New York: Harmony Books, 1999).

Elias, M. J., Zins, J. E., Weissberg, R. P., Frey, K. S., Greenberg, M. T., Haynes, N. M., Kessler, R., Schwab-Stone, M. E., & Shriver, T. P., *Promoting Social and Emotional Learning: Guidelines for Educators* (Alexandria, Vir.: Association for Supervision and Curriculum Development, 1997).

Elliott, D. S., Hamburg, B. A., & Williams, K. R., eds., *Violence in American Schools* (New York: Cambridge University Press, 1998).

Gardner, H., *Multiple Intelligences: The Theory in Practice* (New York: Basic Books, 1993).

Ginott, H., *Between Parent and Child* (New York: Avon, 1969).

Ginott, H., *Between Parent and Teenager* (New York: Avon, 1969).

Goleman, D., *Emotional Intelligence: Why It Can Matter More Than IQ* (New York: Bantam Books, 1995).

Goleman, D., *Working with Emotional Intelligence* (New York: Bantam Books, 1998).

Hechinger, F. M., *Fateful Choices: Healthy Youth for the 21st Century* (New York: Hill and Wang, 1992).

Lantieri, L., & Patti, J., *Waging Peace in Our Schools* (Boston: Beacon Press, 1996).

Lewis, B., *The Kid's Guide to Social Action (Revised Edition)* (Minneapolis: Free Spirit, 1998).

Lewis, B., *The Kid's Guide to Service Projects* (Minneapolis: Free Spirit, 1995).

Mahdi, L., Christopher, N., & Meade, M., eds., *Crossroads: The Quest for Contemporary Rights of Passage* (Chicago: Open Court Press, 1996).

Saarni, C., *The Development of Emotional Competence* (New York: The Guilford Press, 1999).

Salovey, P., & Sluyter, D. J., eds., *Emotional Development and Emotional Intelligence: Educational Implications* (New York: Basic Books, 1997).

Samalin, N., & Whitney, C., *Love and Anger: The Parental Dilemma* (New York: Penguin, 1991).

Schaefer, C. E., & DiGeronimo, T. F., *How to Talk to Teens About Really Important Things* (San Francisco: Jossey-Bass, 1999).

Seligman, M. E. P., *The Optimistic Child* (New York: Harper Perennial, 1995).

Shriver, Maria, *Ten Things I Wish I'd Known—Before I Went Out into the Real World* (New York: Warner Books, 2000).

Wood, C., *Time to Teach, Time to Learn: Changing the Pace of School* (Greenfield, Mass.: Northeast Foundation for Children, 1999).

Recommended Web Sites

www.EQParenting.com
www.iparenting.com (and many linked sites)
www.ivillage.com (Parent Soup)
www.Dr.Koop.com
www.CASEL.org

Index

Emotionally Intelligent Parenting Circles and Networks

Emotionally Intelligent Parenting (EIP) Circles are groups of parents who gather together to read a book and/or discuss a specific topic. The example here will focus on a book. EIP Circles provide participants with a place to learn together, plan together, test ideas together, and reflect together. They work because they allow parents to examine materials, think about and discuss its meaning and importance with other parents, and then apply what they have learned to their everyday parenting.

The Circles also bring the expertise of many parents into the room. You will find that a situation you have difficulty with may well be something that another parent has success with, and so on across all the members. With new ideas from the book and support from other parents as you help each other bring the ideas into your lives, it is much more likely that you will apply what you read and find ways to make it work. Of course, this is especially true for the challenging teenage years.

A key part of EIP Circles is to read the material in a way that is most likely to become useful to you. We include below our guidelines for how to read the material. It's also important to have a structure that people can work with. Most groups of this kind can meet two, three, or four times, especially at first. Sometimes groups are able to meet for a chapter a week or every two weeks, but that may be something to work up to. Don't push it at first. We include below ways to organize the material for both *Emotionally Intelligent Parenting* and *Raising Emotionally Intelligent Teenagers*. Many of the books in our Recommended Readings section also lend themselves well to EIP Circles.

You can organize your EIP Circle around a topic of interest or particular problems you want to solve to concentrate. Obviously, you want broad agreement among members about the book(s) you choose. PTAs and other parent-teacher, home-school organizations are often excellent places from which to organize EIP Circles. It gives these organizations an important role in children's education, building up an area that schools are not quite as expert in as they are in academic content. Holding EIP Circles either just before, just after, or even as the focus of regular meetings makes it more likely that people will attend. Be sure to collect E-mail addresses and phone numbers. In EIP Circles, parents often begin to communicate between meetings, as they start to put ideas into action and find they have questions.

Among the things that help EIP Circles work well is that they are realistic in scheduling, they start and end on time, there is a leader for a particular book, or rotating leadership, that makes sure people know about the next meeting, arranges the logistics, ensures that refreshments are available, and gets the discussion rolling. The optimal group size is six to ten. When it gets much larger, people cannot participate as much. But when this happens, we recommend breaking up into two or more smaller discussion groups, and then coming back toward the end of the meeting to share ideas.

Finally, how an EIP Circle works depends on the group members. Will people conduct themselves with emotional intelligence? Will they listen as others speak? Wait their turn? Avoid giving put-downs? Do the reading that everyone agrees to? Bring any problems into the group, rather than complain outside of it? The interpersonal process is hard to predict and control, but don't give up if the first one or two experiences are a bit rough. Like most things worth doing, EIP Circles take practice, and with practice you all will get better.

An EIP Network consists of EIP Circles that communicate with one another, meet together, etc. PTA's can be especially effective in facilitating these. But so can other organized parent and professional groups, such as parents of ADHD kids, parents of special education students, pediatricians, school psychologists, guidance counselors, and social workers. EIP Networks, especially when facilitated by electronic communications, are ways of bringing extra expertise together on at least an occasional basis.

If you have difficulty, questions, or successes to share, or if you would like help in setting up electronic communications, contact us at www.EQParenting.com.

Outline for Conducting Emotionally Intelligent Parenting Circles

Preliminary Considerations

• What to call it?

Be pragmatic; focus on issues/concerns that parents most want to hear about

Use *Emotionally Intelligent Parenting* in the title to create a thread of continuity

• How many should I have?

Local norms will dictate the answer; most places start with 2 or 3 and rarely do more than 4; spacing greater than every other week loses momentum; if you do 4, once per week, you can expect most people to attend 3 or 4

How to Divide the Material: Emotionally Intelligent Parenting

For a Two-Week Sequence:

> Week #1: Chapters 1 and 2
> Week #2: Chapter 3 *or*
> Chapter 3 and have different people select from
> Chapters 4 or 5

For a Three-Week Sequence:

> Same as two-week series plus either Sound Parenting Bites
> (Chapter 9) or Chapter 7 for Week 3

For a Four-Week Sequence:

> Week #1: Chapters 1 and 2
> Week #2: Chapters 3 and 4

        Week #3: Chapters 5 and 7

        Week #4: Sound Bites & Share Trouble Trackers

How to Divide the Material:
Raising Emotionally Intelligent Teenagers

For a Two-Week Sequence:

        Week #1: Chapters 1 and 2

        Week #2: Chapters 3 and 4

For a Three-Week Sequence:

        Same as two-week series plus Chapter 6 for Week 3

For a Four-Week Sequence:

        Week #1: Chapters 1 and 2

        Week #2: Chapters 3 and 4

        Week #3: Chapters 6

        Week #4: Chapters 7, 8, and/or 9 (at this point, the group
                            may decide to meet for extra time to focus on
                            Chapter 9, and then add Chapter 10)

Guidelines for Reading and for Leading Discussions

3 Revelations

What are three things you read about that you find interesting, new, or thought provoking?

4 Confirmations

What are four things you read that confirm your intuitions or things you are already doing?

3 Emotional Reactions

What are three things you read that you found yourself having an emotional reaction to, either positive or negative (your reactions might have been surprise, embarrassment, annoyance, pride, etc.)?

4 Things That You Will Apply and Where

What are four things you gleaned from your reading that you feel you can and will apply to your own life? Where and how will you do this? What obstacles or roadblocks can you anticipate? How might you get past them? What other resources might help you?

Questions, Comments, Suggestions: Reach us at
www.EQParenting.com